Taste of Home

AMERICA the TASTY

TASTE OF HOME BOOKS • RDA ENTHUSIAST BRANDS, LLC • MILWAUKEE, WI

1610 N. 2nd St., Suite 102
Milwaukee WI 53212-3906

Visit us at **tasteofhome.com** for other Taste of Home books and products.

International Standard Book Number:
979-8-88977-178-4

Content Directors:
Ellie Martin Cliffe, Mark Hagen
Creative Director: Raeann Thompson
Associate Creative Director:
Jami Geittmann
Senior Editor: Christine Rukavena
Senior Art Director: Courtney Lovetere
Manager, Production Design:
Satyandra Raghav
Assistant Art Director:
Jogesh Antony
Senior Print Publication Designer:
Bipin Balakrishnan
Print Production Artist: Nandini Mittal
Deputy Editor, Copy Desk: Ann M. Walter
Contributing Copy Editors:
Nancy J. Stohs, Hazel Wheaton
Contributing Assistant Art Director:
Julie Wagner

Cover Photography
Photographer: Dan Roberts
Set Stylists: Melissa Franco, Stephanie Marchese
Food Stylist: Sarah Farmer

Pictured on front cover:
Patriotic Berry Cream Tart, p. 126

Pictured on back cover:
New England Clam Chowder, p. 8; Fried Chicken, p. 41; Apple Pie, p. 111

Printed in China
1 3 5 7 9 10 8 6 4 2

SLOW-COOKED BLUEBERRY GRUNT, P. 18

CONTENTS

MASSACHUSETTS
NEW ENGLAND
CLAM CHOWDER, P. 8

MASSACHUSETTS
NEW ENGLAND
CLAM CHOWDER, P. 8

CONTENTS

NEW ENGLAND

Yankee thrift meets coastal bounty—here you'll find hearty fare shaped by the seafood favorites and creative traditions of New England's first settlers. Pantry staples, local fruits and the cold-water catch add up to delicious comfort food.

CAPE COD

Simple and delicious, the name tells you all you need to know about this drink. With just two ingredients—vodka and cranberry juice—this Cape Cod cocktail makes for a tart, sweet and sparkling sip.
—Taste of Home *Test Kitchen*

TAKES: 5 MIN. • **MAKES:** 1 SERVING

½ to ¾ cup ice cubes
1½ oz. vodka
3 oz. cranberry juice

GARNISH

Lime twist

Place ice in a highball glass. Pour the vodka and cranberry juice into the glass. Garnish as desired.

1 SERVING 140 cal., 0 fat (0 sat. fat), 0 chol., 4mg sod., 12g carb. (11g sugars, 0 fiber), 0 pro.

INGREDIENT SPOTLIGHT

Massachusetts runs on cranberries—the state berry—and even made cranberry juice its official beverage and cranberry an official state color. The classic Cape Cod (vodka + cranberry) was popularized by Ocean Spray in the 1950s. Puckery, bright and remarkably refreshing—cheers to the Bay State's best-loved berry.

CRUMB-TOPPED CLAMS

In my family, it wouldn't be Christmas Eve without baked clams. However, they make a special bite for any occasion and are easy to make and always a hit. *—Annmarie Lucente*

PREP: 35 MIN. • **BROIL:** 10 MIN.
MAKES: 2 DOZEN

- 2 lbs. kosher salt
- 2 dozen fresh littleneck clams
- ½ cup dry bread crumbs
- ¼ cup chicken broth
- 1 Tbsp. minced fresh parsley
- 2 Tbsp. olive oil
- 2 garlic cloves, minced
- ¼ tsp. dried oregano
- Dash pepper
- 1 Tbsp. panko bread crumbs
- Lemon wedges

1. Spread salt onto a cast-iron 15x10x1-in. baking pan or other ovenproof metal serving platter. Shuck clams, leaving clams and juices in bottom shells. Arrange in prepared pan; divide juices among shells.

2. In a small bowl, mix dry bread crumbs, chicken broth, parsley, oil, garlic, oregano and pepper; spoon over clams. Sprinkle with panko bread crumbs.

3. Broil 4-6 in. from heat until clams are firm and crumb mixture is crisp and golden brown, 6-8 minutes. Serve immediately with lemon wedges.

1 CLAM 31 cal., 1g fat (0 sat. fat), 5mg chol., 35mg sod., 2g carb. (0 sugars, 0 fiber), 2g pro.

NEW ENGLAND CLAM CHOWDER

My recipe makes it easy to enjoy clam chowder any night of the week. Not only are the bits of crispy bacon very traditional, but they also make the soup feel rich and indulgent. —*Amanda Bowyer*

PREP: 20 MIN. • **COOK:** 20 MIN.
MAKES: 7 SERVINGS

- 2 celery ribs, diced
- 2 medium carrots, diced
- 1 medium onion, diced
- 2 tsp. olive oil
- 4 garlic cloves, minced
- 4 medium potatoes, peeled and diced
- 2 cans (6½ oz. each) minced clams, undrained
- 1 bottle (8 oz.) clam juice
- 1 cup plus 1 Tbsp. water, divided
- 1 tsp. minced fresh thyme
- ½ tsp. salt
- ½ tsp. pepper
- 1 can (12 oz.) evaporated milk
- 2 tsp. cornstarch
- 2 bacon strips, cooked and crumbled

1. In a Dutch oven, saute celery, carrots and onion in oil until tender. Add garlic; cook 1 minute longer. Stir in potatoes, clams, clam juice, 1 cup water and seasonings. Bring to a boil. Reduce heat; cover and simmer until potatoes are tender, 12-15 minutes.

2. Gradually stir in milk and heat through. Combine cornstarch and remaining 1 Tbsp. water until smooth; stir into chowder. Bring to a boil; cook and stir for 2 minutes or until thickened. Top with bacon and, if desired, additional fresh thyme.

1 CUP 195 cal., 5g fat (3g sat. fat), 27mg chol., 574mg sod., 28g carb. (8g sugars, 2g fiber), 10g pro.

BROILED LOBSTER TAILS

No matter where you live, these succulent, buttery lobster tails are just a few minutes away. In my home state, we use frozen lobster with delicious results, but if you're near the ocean, by all means use fresh!
—*Lauren McAnelly*

PREP: 30 MIN. • **COOK:** 5 MIN.
MAKES: 4 SERVINGS

- 4 lobster tails (5 to 6 oz. each), thawed
- ¼ cup cold butter, cut into thin slices
- Salt and pepper to taste
- Lemon wedges

1. Preheat broiler. Using kitchen scissors, cut a 2-in.-wide rectangle from the top shell of each lobster tail; loosen from lobster meat and remove.

2. Pull away edges of remaining shell to release lobster meat from sides; pry meat loose from bottom shell, keeping tail end attached. Place in a foil-lined 15x10x1-in. pan. Arrange butter slices over lobster meat.

3. Broil 5-6 in. from heat until meat is opaque, 5-8 minutes. Season with salt and pepper to taste. Serve lobster tails with lemon wedges.

1 LOBSTER TAIL 211 cal., 13g fat (8g sat. fat), 211mg chol., 691mg sod., 0 carb. (0 sugars, 0 fiber), 24g pro.

Recipe may be prepared using a compound herb butter in place of plain butter.

TO MAKE COMPOUND BUTTER
Process ¼ cup softened butter with fresh herbs and seasonings of your choice in a small food processor. Transfer mixture to a sheet of waxed paper; roll into a log, then refrigerate until firm. To use, unwrap and cut into thin slices.

LEMON-CHIVE COMPOUND BUTTER
Add 2 Tbsp. chopped fresh chives, 2 Tbsp. chopped fresh parsley, 1 Tbsp. minced shallot, 1 minced garlic clove, ½ tsp. grated lemon peel and ¼ tsp. salt to butter.

CHIMICHURRI COMPOUND BUTTER
Add 2 Tbsp. chopped fresh cilantro, 2 Tbsp. chopped fresh parsley, 1 Tbsp. minced shallot, 1 tsp. grated lemon peel, 1 tsp. minced fresh oregano, 1 minced garlic clove, ¼ tsp. salt and ⅛ tsp. crushed red pepper flakes to butter.

LOBSTER ROLLS

Mayonnaise infused with dill and lemon lends refreshing flavor to these super sandwiches.
Try pan-toasting the buns in butter for something special.
—Taste of Home *Test Kitchen*

TAKES: 30 MIN.
MAKES: 8 SANDWICHES

- 1 cup chopped celery
- ⅓ cup mayonnaise
- 2 Tbsp. lemon juice
- ½ tsp. dill weed
- 5 cups cubed cooked lobster meat (about 4 small lobsters)
- 8 hoagie rolls, split and toasted

In a large bowl, combine first 4 ingredients. Gently stir in lobster. Serve on rolls.

1 SANDWICH 354 cal., 12g fat (2g sat. fat), 133mg chol., 887mg sod., 36g carb. (5g sugars, 1g fiber), 25g pro.

READER REVIEW

★★★★★

"It has been 40 years since we were in Maine. A highlight, apart from scenery and serenity, was lobster rolls bought along the coastline from lobster shacks. I'm making these tonight for our anniversary dinner. I tasted the mixture before chilling and it was sensational! Using top-split brioche hot dog buns, toasted in butter with dill weed, just like I remember."

—JACKIE185, TASTEOFHOME.COM

TRADITIONAL BOILED DINNER

Corned beef is a frequent treat in our family. We love the savory flavor the vegetables pick up from simmering with the pickling spices.
—Joy Strasser

PREP: 10 MIN. • **COOK:** 2½ HOURS
MAKES: 6 SERVINGS

- 1 corned beef brisket with spice packet (3 lbs.)
- 1 tsp. whole black peppercorns
- 2 bay leaves
- 2 medium potatoes, peeled and quartered
- 3 medium carrots, quartered
- 1 medium onion, cut into 6 wedges
- 1 small head green cabbage, cut into 6 wedges
- Optional: Prepared horseradish or mustard

1. Place the brisket and contents of spice packet in a Dutch oven. Add the peppercorns, bay leaves and enough water to cover; bring to a boil. Reduce heat; cover and simmer for 2 hours or until meat is almost tender.

2. Add potatoes, carrots and onion; bring to a boil. Reduce heat; cover and simmer for 10 minutes. Add cabbage, cover and simmer for 15-20 minutes or until tender. Discard the bay leaves and peppercorns. Thinly slice meat; serve with vegetables and, if desired, horseradish or mustard.

8 OZ. COOKED BEEF WITH VEGETABLES 558 cal., 34g fat (11g sat. fat), 122mg chol., 2797mg sod., 25g carb. (8g sugars, 5g fiber), 37g pro.

BEANIE WEENIES

Beanie weenies (AKA franks and beans) are a longstanding traditional Saturday night supper in New England. My grandmother would make the baked beans and the brown bread served with them from scratch, but now canned varieties of both are available.
—Jolene Martinelli

PREP: 10 MIN. • **COOK:** 25 MIN.
MAKES: 8 SERVINGS

- 1 can (16 oz.) brown bread
- 2 tsp. butter
- 10 hot dogs, sliced
- 1 can (28 oz.) maple and bacon-flavored baked beans

1. Preheat oven to 300°. Slice brown bread into 8 portions; place onto a greased baking sheet. Bake according to package directions.
2. Meanwhile, in a large skillet, melt butter over medium heat. Add hot dog slices; cook and stir until browned. Add baked beans and heat through.
3. Serve in bowls with a slice of baked bread.

1 SERVING 440 cal., 21g fat (8g sat. fat), 41mg chol., 1333mg sod., 48g carb. (1g sugars, 9g fiber), 16g pro.

HEATING OPTIONS

Instead of baking the bread, you can put it in the toaster or fry it on the stovetop in a little butter. Or wrap slices in paper towels and microwave them.

SHEET-PAN NEW ENGLAND CLAMBAKE

This recipe transports you to hot summer nights on the beach enjoying fresh seafood, corn on the cob, spicy sausage and potatoes any time of the year! Bathed in garlicky, spicy butter, this one-pan wonder is beautiful, delicious and easy on cleanup! You could mix up the seafood and add pieces of salmon or haddock, use other quick-cooking veggies like cherry tomatoes or asparagus or substitute kielbasa for the chorizo. It's so versatile!
—Pamela Gelsomini

PREP: 25 MIN. • **BAKE:** 45 MIN.
MAKES: 6 SERVINGS

- 1 lb. assorted baby potatoes
- 2 Tbsp. olive oil
- 2 tsp. Italian seasoning
- 6 half-ears frozen corn on the cob, thawed
- 2 lbs. fresh mussels, scrubbed and beards removed
- 1½ dozen fresh littleneck clams, scrubbed
- 1 lb. uncooked shrimp (26-30 per lb.), peeled and deveined
- ½ lb. fully cooked Spanish or Portuguese chorizo links, cut into ½-in. pieces
- ¼ cup dry white wine or chicken broth
- 1 medium lemon, cut into wedges
- ½ cup butter, melted
- 4 garlic cloves, chopped
- 2 tsp. seafood seasoning
- 1¼ tsp. Cajun seasoning
- ¼ tsp. pepper
- 2 Tbsp. minced fresh parsley
- French bread, optional

1. Preheat oven to 400°. Place potatoes in a 15x10x1-in. baking pan. Drizzle with oil and sprinkle with Italian seasoning; toss to coat. Bake until tender, 25-30 minutes. Using a potato masher, flatten potatoes to ½-in. thickness; remove and keep warm.

2. Add corn, mussels, clams, shrimp and chorizo to same pan; top with potatoes. Pour wine into pan. Squeeze lemon wedges over top; add to pan.

3. Combine butter, garlic, seafood seasoning and Cajun seasoning. Pour half the butter mixture over the top. Bake until shrimp turn pink and mussels and clams open, 20-25 minutes. Discard any unopened mussels or clams.

4. Drizzle with remaining butter mixture. Sprinkle with pepper; top with parsley. If desired, serve with bread.

1 SERVING 639 cal., 35g fat (15g sat. fat), 214mg chol., 1302mg sod., 37g carb. (4g sugars, 3g fiber), 46g pro.

OCEAN STATE CLAMBAKE

Rhode Island keeps the classic clambake—a Wampanoag seaside cooking tradition shared with English settlers—very much alive, from Newport beaches to backyard pots. Rhode Islanders steam their clams and mussels with corn, red potatoes, onions and smoky Portuguese chorizo (plus shrimp and even lobsters).

VERMONT CHICKEN PIE

This potpie topped with homemade biscuits is oh-so-comforting. It's a real family favorite.
—Marcy Schewe

PREP: 1 HOUR • **BAKE:** 20 MIN.
MAKES: 8 SERVINGS

- 1 broiler/fryer chicken (3 to 3½ lbs.), quartered
- 4 cups water
- 3 medium carrots, halved widthwise
- 2 medium onions
- 4 tsp. chicken bouillon granules
- 1 bay leaf
- ½ lb. fresh mushrooms, quartered
- 2 celery ribs, halved widthwise
- 3 Tbsp. butter
- 5 Tbsp. all-purpose flour
- ½ cup heavy whipping cream
- 1 tsp. poultry seasoning
- 1 tsp. salt
- ¼ tsp. pepper
- 1 cup frozen peas

BISCUITS

- 1½ cups all-purpose flour
- 2 tsp. baking powder
- 1¼ tsp. sugar
- ¼ tsp. salt
- 5 Tbsp. shortening
- ½ cup milk

1. In a Dutch oven, combine first 6 ingredients; bring to a boil. Reduce heat; cover and simmer 20 minutes. Add mushrooms and celery; cover and simmer for 15 minutes or until chicken and vegetables are tender.

2. Remove chicken and vegetables. Debone chicken; dice meat. Slice vegetables. Strain broth, reserving 2 cups. (Discard remaining broth or save for another use.)

3. Melt butter in a large saucepan; stir in flour until smooth. Gradually stir in cream and reserved broth; bring to a boil. Cook and stir for 2 minutes or until thickened and bubbly. Add the poultry seasoning, salt, pepper, peas and reserved chicken and vegetables. Pour into a 2-qt. round baking dish. Set aside and keep warm.

4. For biscuits, combine the flour, baking powder, sugar and salt. Cut in shortening until mixture resembles coarse crumbs. Stir in milk just until moistened. On a floured surface, roll out to ½-in. thickness. Cut with a 2½-in. biscuit cutter. Place biscuits over chicken mixture. Bake at 400° 20 minutes or until biscuits are golden brown.

1 SERVING 538 cal., 31g fat (12g sat. fat), 108mg chol., 1064mg sod., 32g carb. (5g sugars, 3g fiber), 31g pro.

A CHURCH-SUPPER CLASSIC

Vermont chicken pie is pure comfort food: tender chicken and rich gravy under a layer of fluffy biscuits. Many Vermonters serve their veggies on the side, rather than cluttering up the chicken-and-gravy filling.

SAUSAGE JOHNNYCAKE

Here's a nice, hearty breakfast with plenty of old-fashioned flavor. I serve it to my bed-and-breakfast customers who love the cake's savory middle and the maple syrup topping. It's a great way to start the day!
—Lorraine Guyn

PREP: 20 MIN. • **BAKE:** 30 MIN.
MAKES: 6 SERVINGS

- 1 cup cornmeal
- 2 cups buttermilk
- 12 uncooked breakfast sausage links
- 1⅓ cups all-purpose flour
- ¼ cup sugar
- 1½ tsp. baking powder
- ½ tsp. baking soda
- ½ tsp. salt
- ⅓ cup shortening
- 1 large egg, lightly beaten
- ½ tsp. vanilla extract
- Maple syrup

1. Preheat oven to 400°. In a small bowl, combine the cornmeal and buttermilk; let stand for 10 minutes.
2. Meanwhile, in a 9-in. cast-iron skillet over medium heat, cook sausage until no longer pink; drain on paper towels. Arrange 8 links in a spokelike pattern in same skillet or in a greased 9-in. deep-dish pie plate. Cut remaining links in half; place between whole sausages.
3. In a large bowl, combine flour, sugar, baking powder, baking soda and salt. Cut in shortening until mixture resembles coarse crumbs.
4. Stir egg and vanilla into cornmeal mixture; add to dry ingredients and stir just until blended. Pour batter over sausages.
5. Bake until a toothpick inserted in the center comes out clean, 30-35 minutes. Serve warm with syrup.

FREEZE OPTION Wrap baked cake in foil; transfer to a freezer container. Freeze for up to 3 months. To use frozen cake, remove foil and thaw at room temperature. Serve warm with syrup.

1 PIECE 481 cal., 23g fat (7g sat. fat), 64mg chol., 940mg sod., 53g carb. (13g sugars, 2g fiber), 15g pro.

INGREDIENT SPOTLIGHT

Vermont is America's top maple-syrup producer, sugaring 890,000 gallons per year. New York and Maine occupy the second and third spots. Syrup made early in the season—the golden and amber grades—is best for drizzling over johnnycake and flapjacks. Dark and very dark syrups give intense maple flavor to recipes.

SPICED ACORN SQUASH

Working full time, I found I didn't always have time to cook the meals my family loved. So I re-created many of those dishes in the slow cooker. This treatment for squash is one of our favorites.
—Carol Greco

PREP: 15 MIN. • **COOK:** 3½ HOURS
MAKES: 4 SQUASH HALVES

- ¾ cup packed brown sugar
- 1 tsp. ground cinnamon
- 1 tsp. ground nutmeg
- 2 small acorn squash, halved and seeded
- ¾ cup raisins
- 4 Tbsp. butter
- ½ cup water

1. In a small bowl, mix brown sugar, cinnamon and nutmeg; spoon into squash halves. Sprinkle with the raisins. Top each with 1 Tbsp. butter. Wrap each half individually in heavy- duty foil, sealing tightly.
2. Pour water into a 5-qt. slow cooker. Place squash in slow cooker, cut side up (packets may be stacked). Cook, covered, on high 3½-4 hours or until squash is tender. Open foil carefully to allow steam to escape.
1 SQUASH HALF 433 cal., 12g fat (7g sat. fat), 31mg chol., 142mg sod., 86g carb. (63g sugars, 5g fiber), 3g pro.

POPOVERS

Popovers are a Christmas morning tradition my father-in-law started more than 30 years ago. Now I get up early to make them, then wake the family to begin opening gifts. When the popovers are ready, I serve them with lots of butter and assorted jams.
—Sue Jurack

PREP: 15 MIN. • **BAKE:** 35 MIN.
MAKES: 9 POPOVERS

- 1¼ cups whole milk, room temperature
- 1 Tbsp. butter, melted and cooled
- 1 cup all-purpose flour
- ¼ tsp. salt
- 2 large eggs, room temperature

1. In a small bowl, beat the milk, butter, flour and salt until blended. Add eggs, 1 at a time, beating well after each addition. Fill buttered popover pans or large custard cups three-fourths full.
2. Bake at 450° for 15 minutes. Reduce heat to 350°; bake until very firm, about 20 minutes longer. Remove from the oven and prick each popover with a sharp knife to allow steam to escape. Serve immediately.
1 POPOVER 99 cal., 4g fat (2g sat. fat), 55mg chol., 109mg sod., 12g carb. (2g sugars, 0 fiber), 4g pro.

AUTHENTIC BOSTON BROWN BREAD

The rustic, old-fashioned flavor of this hearty bread is out of this world. Recipes like this remind me why I find cooking and baking not only fun, but very fulfilling.
—Sharon Delaney-Chronis

PREP: 20 MIN.
COOK: 50 MIN. + STANDING
MAKES: 1 LOAF (12 PIECES)

- ½ cup cornmeal
- ½ cup whole wheat flour
- ½ cup rye flour
- ½ tsp. baking powder
- ½ tsp. baking soda
- ¼ tsp. salt
- 1 cup buttermilk
- ⅓ cup molasses
- 2 Tbsp. brown sugar
- 1 Tbsp. canola oil
- 3 Tbsp. chopped walnuts, toasted
- 3 Tbsp. raisins
- Cream cheese, softened, optional

1. In a large bowl, combine the first 6 ingredients. In another bowl, whisk buttermilk, molasses, brown sugar and oil. Stir into the dry ingredients just until moistened. Fold in walnuts and raisins. Transfer to a greased 8x4-in. loaf pan; cover with foil.

2. Place pan on a rack in a boiling-water canner or other large, deep pot; add 1 in. hot water to pot. Bring to a gentle boil; cover and steam for 45-50 minutes or until a toothpick inserted in the center comes out clean, adding more water to pot as needed.

3. Remove pan from pot; let stand for 10 minutes before removing bread from pan to a wire rack. Serve with cream cheese if desired.

1 PIECE 124 cal., 3g fat (0 sat. fat), 1mg chol., 145mg sod., 23g carb. (10g sugars, 2g fiber), 3g pro.

ORIGIN STORY

New England cooks stretched their precious wheat with rye and corn flours, then steamed the dough in molds (or coffee cans) when ovens were scarce. The result: moist, subtly sweet Boston brown bread—a classic alongside baked beans or homemade soup.

SLOW-COOKED BLUEBERRY GRUNT

If you love blueberries, then you can't go wrong with this easy slow-cooked dessert. For a special treat, serve it warm with vanilla ice cream.
—*Cleo Gonske*

PREP: 20 MIN. • **COOK:** 2½ HOURS
MAKES: 6 SERVINGS

- 4 cups fresh or frozen blueberries
- ¾ cup sugar
- ½ cup water
- 1 tsp. almond extract

DUMPLINGS

- 2 cups all-purpose flour
- 4 tsp. baking powder
- 1 tsp. sugar
- ½ tsp. salt
- 1 Tbsp. cold butter
- 1 Tbsp. shortening
- ¾ cup 2% milk
- Vanilla ice cream, optional

1. Place blueberries, sugar, water and extract in a 3-qt. slow cooker; stir to combine. Cook, covered, on high 2-3 hours or until bubbly.

2. For dumplings, in a small bowl, whisk flour, baking powder, sugar and salt. Cut in the butter and shortening until crumbly. Add milk; stir just until a soft dough forms.

3. Drop dough by tablespoonfuls on top of hot blueberry mixture. Cook, covered, 30 minutes longer or until a toothpick inserted in center of dumplings comes out clean. If desired, serve warm with ice cream.

1 CUP 360 cal., 5g fat (2g sat. fat), 7mg chol., 494mg sod., 73g carb. (37g sugars, 3g fiber), 6g pro.

PEAR PANDOWDY

I pulled out this recipe one night when my husband was craving something sweet, and it was a big hit with both of us. It's a superb last-minute dessert that almost melts in your mouth.
—Jennifer Class

PREP: 20 MIN. • **BAKE:** 20 MIN.
MAKES: 2 SERVINGS

- 2 medium firm pears, peeled and sliced
- 2 Tbsp. brown sugar
- 4½ tsp. butter
- 1½ tsp. lemon juice
- ⅛ tsp. ground cinnamon
- ⅛ tsp. ground nutmeg

TOPPING

- ½ cup all-purpose flour
- 2 Tbsp. plus ½ tsp. sugar
- ½ tsp. baking powder
- ⅛ tsp. salt
- ¼ cup cold butter, cubed
- 2 Tbsp. water
- Vanilla ice cream, optional

1. In a small saucepan, combine the first 6 ingredients. Cook and stir over medium heat until pears are tender, about 5 minutes. Pour into a greased 3-cup baking dish.

2. In a small bowl, combine the flour, 2 Tbsp. sugar, baking powder and salt; cut in butter until crumbly. Stir in water. Sprinkle over pear mixture. Sprinkle with remaining ½ tsp. sugar.

3. Bake, uncovered, at 375° until a toothpick inserted into topping comes out clean and topping is lightly browned, 20-25 minutes. Serve warm, with ice cream if desired.

1 SERVING 594 cal., 32g fat (20g sat. fat), 84mg chol., 572mg sod., 76g carb. (45g sugars, 5g fiber), 4g pro.

ORIGIN STORY

One theory behind the name of this fruity deep-dish treat is that it comes from the dish's rather plain and dowdy appearance. Brown sugar or molasses (which was far cheaper than refined white sugar used to be) is the traditional sweetener in this thrifty dessert.

MARYLAND
EASY CRAB
CAKES,
P. 30

MIDDLE ATLANTIC STATES

Where ocean harbors give way to rolling farm country, you'll find tasty foods inspired by boardwalks, big cities, rural towns and the Chesapeake's catch. This tour spans Capitol lunch-counter fare, Italian-American "gravy" and from-scratch Amish favorites.

LONG ISLAND ICED TEA

Smooth but potent describes this drink. Adjust the tequila to suit your taste. If you like a bold flavor, use an ounce. If you like a more mellow drink, use half an ounce.
—Taste of Home *Test Kitchen*

TAKES: 5 MIN. • **MAKES:** 1 SERVING

- 1 to 1¼ cups ice cubes
- 1 oz. vodka
- 1 oz. gin
- 1 oz. light rum
- 1 oz. sour mix
- 1 oz. triple sec
- ½ to 1 oz. tequila
- ½ oz. cola
- Lemon slice, optional

Place ice in a Collins or highball glass. Pour the next 7 ingredients into the glass; stir. If desired, garnish with a slice of lemon.
⅔ CUP 330 cal., 0 fat (0 sat. fat), 0 chol., 3mg sod., 30g carb. (28g sugars, 0 fiber), 0 pro.

ORIGIN STORY

Created on Long Island's South Shore at the Oak Beach Inn in Suffolk County, legendary Long Island Iced Tea was a 1970s bartenders' contest winner. A blend of five different spirits masquerade as "iced tea" when a splash of brown cola is added. Sour mix lends a lemony tartness. OBI bartender Robert "Rosebud" Butt is generally credited as the creator, though his co-worker, Chris Bendicksen, is sometimes cited.

ANTIPASTO SKEWERS

This elegant-looking appetizer is quick and easy to make. It's perfect for dinner parties, cocktail parties and everything in between!
—*Amanda Pederson*

TAKES: 15 MIN. • **MAKES:** 1 DOZEN

- 24 grape tomatoes (about 1 pint)
- 1 carton (8 oz.) cherry-size fresh mozzarella cheese
- 12 thin slices hard salami (about ¼ lb.)
- 12 pimiento-stuffed Queen olives
- Italian vinaigrette, optional

On 12 wooden 6-in. skewers, alternately thread tomatoes, mozzarella, folded salami slices and olives. Refrigerate until serving. If desired, drizzle skewers with vinaigrette before serving.
1 SKEWER 204 cal., 9g fat (4g sat. fat), 24mg chol., 345mg sod., 24g carb. (16g sugars, 7g fiber), 11g pro.

CRISPY BUFFALO WINGS

Coating the wings with baking powder helps crisp them up in the oven. These are doused in Buffalo sauce, but could also be brushed with your favorite barbecue sauce instead.
—Taste of Home *Test Kitchen*

PREP: 15 MIN. • **BAKE:** 40 MIN.
MAKES: ABOUT 20 PIECES

- 2 Tbsp. butter, melted
- 1 Tbsp. vegetable oil
- 2 lbs. chicken wings
- 2 Tbsp. baking powder
- 1 tsp. salt
- 1 tsp. garlic powder

SAUCE

- ¼ cup butter, cubed
- ½ cup Louisiana-style hot sauce
- 2 tsp. brown sugar

1. Preheat oven to 425°. Line a 15x10x1-in. baking pan with foil or parchment. Pour butter and oil over foil; brush to coat evenly.
2. Using a sharp knife, cut through the 2 wing joints; discard wing tips. In a large bowl, combine baking powder, salt and garlic powder; add wing pieces, a few at a time, and toss to coat; shake off excess.
3. Place on prepared baking sheet. Bake until golden brown, 30-35 minutes.
4. Meanwhile, in a small saucepan, combine sauce ingredients over medium heat. Cook and stir until sugar is dissolved.
5. Brush wings with half the sauce. Cook until browned and juices run clear, 8-10 minutes longer. Brush with remaining sauce.

1 PIECE 89 cal., 7g fat (3g sat. fat), 24mg chol., 532mg sod., 1g carb. (0 sugars, 0 fiber), 5g pro.

INGREDIENT SPOTLIGHT

Louisiana-style hot sauce—like Frank's RedHot—is a thin, tangy blend of aged cayenne peppers, vinegar, water, salt and garlic. It's mildly spicy, bringing bright, tangy heat without being overwhelming. For Buffalo wings, it's enriched with melted butter and tossed with the hot, crispy chicken.

CHEWY SOFT PRETZELS

These homemade pretzels never last long around our house. My kids love to make them and eat them! I serve them to company with dips such as pizza sauce, ranch dressing, spinach dip or hot mustard.
—Elvira Martens

PREP: 1 HOUR + RISING
BAKE: 15 MIN. • **MAKES:** 1 DOZEN

- 1 pkg. (¼ oz.) active dry yeast
- 1½ cups warm water (110° to 115°)
- 1 Tbsp. sugar
- 2 tsp. salt
- 4 to 4¼ cups all-purpose flour
- 8 cups water
- ½ cup baking soda
- 1 large egg, lightly beaten
  Optional toppings: Kosher salt, sesame seeds, poppy seeds and grated Parmesan cheese

1. In a bowl, dissolve yeast in warm water. In a large bowl, combine sugar, salt, yeast mixture and 2 cups flour; beat on medium speed until smooth. Stir in enough of the remaining 2-2 ¼ cups flour to form a stiff dough.

2. Turn out dough onto a floured surface; knead until smooth and elastic, about 5 minutes. Place in a greased bowl, turning once to grease the top. Cover and let rise in a warm place until doubled, about 1 hour.

3. Punch down dough; divide and shape into 12 balls. Roll each into a 22-in. rope and shape into a pretzel.

4. Preheat oven to 425°. Place the water and baking soda in a large saucepan; bring to a boil. Place pretzels, 1 at a time, in boiling water for 30 seconds. Remove and drain on paper towels that have been lightly coated with cooking spray.

5. Place pretzels on greased baking sheets. Brush with egg; top as desired. Bake until golden brown, 12-14 minutes. Remove from pans to wire racks; serve warm.

1 PRETZEL 164 cal., 1g fat (0 sat. fat), 16mg chol., 400mg sod., 33g carb. (1g sugars, 1g fiber), 5g pro.

READER REVIEW

"Instead of shaping them into a pretzel shape, I made pretzel nuggets buy rolling them into strips and cutting them into 1½-in. pieces. Great recipe for pretzels!"
—ANGEL182009, TASTEOFHOME.COM

DISCO FRIES

Disco fries are New Jersey's version of poutine. You can find them at diners when you're in need of a late-night bite, or anytime you've got a craving for a hearty, savory snack.
—Melissa Gaman

PREP: 15 MIN. • **COOK:** 30 MIN.
MAKES: 4 SERVINGS

- 4 cups frozen french-fried potatoes (about 1 lb.)
- 3 Tbsp. unsalted butter
- ¼ cup chopped shallot
- 3 Tbsp. all-purpose flour
- 1½ cups reduced-sodium beef broth
- 2 tsp. Worcestershire sauce
- ½ tsp. pepper
- ¼ tsp. salt
- 6 oz. mozzarella cheese
- 2 Tbsp. thinly sliced green onions

1. Bake french fries according to package directions; add 10-15 minutes to the baking time or bake until very crispy, tossing occasionally.

2. Meanwhile, melt butter in a small saucepan over medium heat. Add shallot; cook, stirring frequently, until softened and browned, about 2 minutes. Add flour; whisk until smooth. Cook until roux is lightly browned, 1-2 minutes. Reduce heat to medium-low; slowly whisk in beef broth until smooth. Add Worcestershire, pepper and salt. Simmer, whisking occasionally, until the gravy has thickened enough to coat the back of a spoon, about 6-8 minutes. Keep warm.

3. Grate 4 oz. mozzarella on the large holes of a box grater. Cut remaining mozzarella into small cubes. Top fries with shredded and cubed cheese. Return to the oven and bake until cheese is just melted, 4-5 minutes.

4. Divide fries among 4 plates; generously top with the gravy. Sprinkle with green onions. Serve extra gravy on the side if desired. Serve immediately.

1 SERVING 404 cal., 24g fat (12g sat. fat), 58mg chol., 1002mg sod., 34g carb. (3g sugars, 3g fiber), 14g pro.

HUNGRY AT THE DISCO

Gorgeous golden heaps of crinkle-cut fries blanketed in melted mozzarella and beef gravy are a perfect pick-me-up in New Jersey, diner capital of the world. Famously, they first fueled famished club-goers in the 1970s.

PICKLED EGGS WITH BEETS

Ever since I can remember, my mother served pickled eggs at Easter. My family expected them. I made them for my granddaughter the last time she visited, and they were all gone before she left.
—Mary Banker

PREP: 10 MIN. + CHILLING
MAKES: 12 SERVINGS

- 2 cans (15 oz. each) whole beets
- 12 hard-boiled large eggs, peeled
- 1 cup sugar
- 1 cup water
- 1 cup cider vinegar

1. Drain beets, reserving 1 cup juice (discard remaining juice or save for another use). Place beets and eggs in a 2-qt. glass jar.
2. In a small saucepan, bring the sugar, water, vinegar and reserved beet juice to a boil. Pour over beets and eggs; cool.
3. Cover tightly and refrigerate for at least 24 hours before serving.
1 SERVING 106 cal., 5g fat (2g sat. fat), 187mg chol., 200mg sod., 7g carb. (6g sugars, 1g fiber), 7g pro.

EYE-CATCHING AMISH EGGS

Pennsylvania Dutch (Amish) cooks pickle hard-boiled eggs with red beets, vinegar, sugar and spices. The beets tint the whites a vivid fuchsia and add a sweet-sour snap. Slice the eggs onto salads or, at Easter, mash the yolks and refill the beet-blushed whites for pink deviled eggs.

AMISH CHICKEN CORN SOUP

Creamed corn and butter make my chicken noodle soup homey and rich. This recipe makes a big batch, but the soup freezes well for future meals.
—Beverly Hoffman

PREP: 15 MIN. • **COOK:** 50 MIN.
MAKES: 12 SERVINGS (ABOUT 4 QT.)

- 1 medium onion, chopped
- 2 celery ribs, chopped
- 1 cup shredded carrots
- 2 lbs. boneless skinless chicken breasts, cubed
- 3 chicken bouillon cubes
- 1 tsp. salt
- ¼ tsp. pepper
- 12 cups water
- 2 cups uncooked egg noodles
- 2 cans (14¾ oz. each) cream-style corn
- ¼ cup butter
- Optional: Celery leaves and coarsely ground pepper

1. Place first 8 ingredients in a Dutch oven; bring slowly to a boil. Reduce heat; simmer, uncovered, until chicken is no longer pink and vegetables are tender, about 30 minutes.
2. Stir in noodles, corn and butter. Cook, uncovered, until noodles are tender, about 10 minutes, stirring occasionally. If desired, top with celery leaves and pepper.
1⅓ CUPS 201 cal., 6g fat (3g sat. fat), 57mg chol., 697mg sod., 19g carb. (3g sugars, 2g fiber), 18g pro.

U.S. SENATE BEAN SOUP

Chock-full of ham, beans and celery, this hearty soup makes a wonderful meal at any time of year. Freeze the bone from a holiday ham until you're ready to make soup. Once prepared, it freezes well for a wonderful make-ahead supper!
—*Rosemarie Forcum*

PREP: 30 MIN. + STANDING
COOK: 3¾ HOURS + COOLING
MAKES: 10 SERVINGS (2½ QT.)

- 1 lb. dried great northern beans or dried navy beans
- 1 meaty ham bone or 2 smoked ham hocks
- 3 medium onions, chopped
- 3 garlic cloves, minced
- 3 celery ribs, chopped
- ¼ cup minced fresh parsley
- 1 cup mashed potatoes or ⅓ cup instant potato flakes
- Salt and pepper to taste
- Minced parsley or chives

1. Rinse and sort beans. Place beans in a Dutch oven or soup kettle; add water to cover by 2 in. Bring to a boil; boil for 2 minutes. Remove from heat; cover and let stand for 1-4 hours or until beans are softened.

2. Drain and rinse beans, discarding liquid. In a large Dutch oven or soup kettle, place the beans, ham bone or hocks and 3 qt. water. Bring to a boil. Reduce heat; cover and simmer for 2 hours.

3. Skim off fat if necessary. Add the onions, garlic, celery, parsley, potatoes, salt and pepper; simmer 1 hour longer.

4. Set aside ham bones until cool enough to handle. Remove meat from bones; discard bones. Cut meat into bite-sized pieces and return to Dutch oven. Heat through. Sprinkle with parsley or chives.

1 CUP 219 cal., 3g fat (1g sat. fat), 11mg chol., 342mg sod., 36g carb. (3g sugars, 10g fiber), 15g pro.

CAPITOL CLASSIC

Served daily in the U.S. Senate's restaurant since the early 1900s, this simple, hearty bean soup is a Capitol Hill constant. Credit for the tradition toggles between Senators Fred Dubois (D.—Idaho) and Knute Nelson (R.—Minnesota). Either way, the order stuck as something both parties could agree on.

SLOW-COOKER SPAGHETTI & MEATBALLS

I've been cooking for 50 years, and this dish is still one that guests request frequently. It is my No. 1 standby recipe and also makes amazing meatball sandwiches. The sauce works for any type of pasta.
—Jane Whittaker

PREP: 50 MIN. • **COOK:** 5 HOURS
MAKES: 12 SERVINGS

- 1 cup seasoned bread crumbs
- 2 Tbsp. grated Parmesan and Romano cheese blend
- 1 tsp. pepper
- ½ tsp. salt
- 2 large eggs, lightly beaten
- 2 lbs. ground beef

SAUCE

- 1 large onion, finely chopped
- 1 medium green pepper, finely chopped
- 3 cans (15 oz. each) tomato sauce
- 2 cans (14½ oz. each) diced tomatoes, undrained
- 1 can (6 oz.) tomato paste
- 6 garlic cloves, minced
- 2 bay leaves
- 1 tsp. each dried basil, oregano and parsley flakes
- 1 tsp. salt
- ½ tsp. pepper
- ¼ tsp. crushed red pepper flakes
- Hot cooked spaghetti

1. In a large bowl, mix bread crumbs, cheese, pepper and salt; stir in eggs. Add beef; mix lightly but thoroughly. Shape into 1½-in. balls. In a large skillet, brown meatballs in batches over medium heat; drain.
2. Place first 5 sauce ingredients in a 6-qt. slow cooker; stir in garlic and seasonings. Add meatballs, stirring gently to coat. Cook, covered, on low for 5-6 hours or until meatballs are cooked through.
3. Discard bay leaves. Serve meatballs and sauce with spaghetti.

ABOUT 3 MEATBALLS WITH ¾ CUP SAUCE 250 cal., 11g fat (4g sat. fat), 79mg chol., 1116mg sod., 20g carb. (7g sugars, 4g fiber), 20g pro.

READER REVIEW

★★★★★

"I make this recipe often, especially during the cold winter months. Over the years, I have added a carrot to the ingredient list. This addition comes from my Italian mother-in-law. The carrot adds natural sweetness. Just remove the carrot before serving."

—LORETTALIB, TASTEOFHOME.COM

EASY CRAB CAKES

Ready-to-go crabmeat makes these delicate patties ideal for dinner when you are pressed for time. You can also form the crab mixture into four thick patties instead of eight cakes.
—Charlene Spelock

TAKES: 25 MIN.
MAKES: 4 SERVINGS

- 1 cup seasoned bread crumbs, divided
- 2 green onions, finely chopped
- ¼ cup finely chopped sweet red pepper
- 1 large egg, lightly beaten
- ¼ cup reduced-fat mayonnaise
- 1 Tbsp. lemon juice
- ½ tsp. garlic powder
- ⅛ tsp. cayenne pepper
- 2 cans (6 oz. each) crabmeat, drained, flaked and cartilage removed
- 1 Tbsp. butter

1. In a large bowl, combine ⅓ cup bread crumbs, green onions, red pepper, egg, mayonnaise, lemon juice, garlic powder and cayenne; fold in crab.

2. Place remaining bread crumbs in a shallow bowl. Divide crab mixture into 8 portions; shape into 2-in. balls. Gently coat with the bread crumbs and shape into ½-in.-thick patties.

3. In a large nonstick skillet, heat butter over medium-high heat. Add crab cakes; cook until golden brown, 3-4 minutes on each side.

2 CRAB CAKES 239 cal., 11g fat (3g sat. fat), 141mg chol., 657mg sod., 13g carb. (2g sugars, 1g fiber), 21g pro.

CUSTOMIZE YOUR CRAB CAKES

• **Cracker binding.** Choose buttery Ritz or simple saltine cracker crumbs as a binder instead of breadcrumbs. They add just-right salt, light crunch and a tender texture—in the classic Maryland style.

• **Chesapeake Bay seasoning.** Swap the cayenne for Old Bay or other seafood seasoning. A light sprinkle on top adds a pop of color too.

• **Fresh herbs.** Fold in minced parsley or chives for a clean herbal note to brighten the crab.

PHILLY CHEESESTEAK SANDWICHES FROM THE SLOW COOKER

These sandwiches are melt-in-your-mouth delicious! Everybody loves a good cheesesteak smothered with onions and peppers, then topped with cheese.
—Kimberly Wallace, Dennison, OH

PREP: 15 MIN. • **COOK:** 7 HOURS
MAKES: 8 SERVINGS

- 1 beef top sirloin steak (3 lbs.), thinly sliced
- 2 large onions, cut into ½-in. strips
- 1 can (10½ oz.) condensed French onion soup, undiluted
- 2 garlic cloves, minced
- 1 pkg. Italian salad dressing mix
- 2 tsp. beef base
- ½ tsp. pepper
- 2 large red or green peppers, cut into ½-in. strips
- ½ cup pickled pepper rings
- 8 hoagie buns or French rolls, split
- 8 slices provolone cheese

1. Combine the first 7 ingredients in a 4- or 5-qt. slow cooker. Cook, covered, on low for 6 hours. Stir in peppers and pepper rings; cover and cook 1-2 hours longer or until meat is tender..

2. Place bun bottoms on ungreased baking sheets, cut sides up. Using tongs, top with beef, vegetables and cheese. Broil 3-4 in. from heat until cheese is melted, 1-2 minutes. Add bun tops; serve with cooking juices.

NOTE Look for beef base near the broth and bouillon.

1 SANDWICH 547 cal., 18g fat (7g sat. fat), 85mg chol., 1381mg sod., 45g carb. (10g sugars, 3g fiber), 51g pro.

PHILLY LORE, EXPLORED

Restaurateur brothers Pat and Harry Olivieri created the steak sandwich; a clever manager slid on the melty provolone—and the beloved Philly Cheesesteak was born. Today at Pat's King of Steaks in Philadelphia, you can choose your melt: the traditional provolone, silky Cheez Whiz, or Cooper Sharp American.

MARYLAND CORN POPS

Fresh-picked sweet corn is a big thing in Maryland. Here's my homespun version of Mexican street corn that brings in local Bay flavors.
—Kristie Schley

PREP: 25 MIN. • **GRILL:** 10 MIN.
MAKES: 2 DOZEN

- 8 medium ears sweet corn, husked
- 2 Tbsp. canola oil
- 1½ cups mayonnaise
- 1½ tsp. garlic powder
- ¼ tsp. freshly ground pepper
- 24 corncob holders
- 2 cups crumbled feta cheese
- 2 Tbsp. seafood seasoning
- ¼ cup minced fresh cilantro
- Lime wedges, optional

1. Brush all sides of corn with oil. Grill, covered, over medium heat until tender and lightly browned, 10-12 minutes, turning occasionally. Remove from grill; cool slightly.
2. Meanwhile, in a small bowl, mix mayonnaise, garlic powder and pepper. Cut each ear of corn into thirds. Insert 1 corncob holder into each piece. Spread corn with mayonnaise mixture; sprinkle with cheese, seafood seasoning and cilantro. If desired, serve with lime wedges.

1 CORN POP 164 cal., 14g fat (3g sat. fat), 10mg chol., 336mg sod., 7g carb. (2g sugars, 1g fiber), 3g pro.

GARLIC KNOTS

These golden garlic knots are bursting at the seams with savory flavors. They're so delicious that your family might enjoy them more than the main course!
—Margaret Knoebel

PREP: 20 MIN. + RISING
BAKE: 10 MIN. • **MAKES:** 2 DOZEN

- 3 to 3¼ cups all-purpose flour
- 1 pkg. (¼ oz.) quick-rise yeast
- 1 Tbsp. sugar
- 1 tsp. salt
- ¾ cup 2% milk
- ¼ cup water
- ¾ cup butter plus 1 Tbsp. butter, divided
- 3 Tbsp. grated Parmesan cheese
- 1 Tbsp. minced garlic
- 1 tsp. dried oregano
- 1 tsp. dried parsley flakes
- ¼ tsp. kosher salt

1. Combine 1½ cups flour, yeast, sugar and salt. In a small saucepan, heat milk, ¼ cup water and 1 Tbsp. butter to 120°-130°. Add to dry ingredients; beat on medium speed just until moistened. Stir in enough remaining flour to form a stiff dough.

2. Turn out dough onto a lightly floured surface; knead until smooth and elastic, 6-8 minutes. Place in a greased bowl, turning once to grease the top. Cover and let rise in a warm place until doubled, about 45 minutes.

3. Punch down dough. Divide into 24 pieces. Roll each piece into a 4-in. rope and tie into a knot; tuck ends under. Place 2 in. apart on a greased baking sheet. Cover and let rise for 15 minutes.

4. Preheat oven to 400°. Bake until golden brown, 8-10 minutes.

5. In a small saucepan, combine remaining ¾ cup butter, garlic, oregano, parsley and salt. Cook over medium heat until butter melts and garlic becomes fragrant. Transfer to a large bowl. Add warm garlic knots and Parmesan; gently toss to coat.

1 PIECE 126 cal., 7g fat (4g sat. fat), 19mg chol., 187mg sod., 13g carb. (1g sugars, 1g fiber), 2g pro.

SHOOFLY PIE

My grandmother made the best shoofly pie in the tradition of the Pennsylvania Dutch. Shoofly pie is to the Amish as pecan pie is to a Southerner.
—Mark Morgan

PREP: 20 MIN. + CHILLING
BAKE: 65 MIN. + COOLING
MAKES: 8 SERVINGS

- Dough for single-crust pie
- ½ cup packed brown sugar
- ½ cup molasses
- 1 large egg
- 1½ tsp. all-purpose flour
- ½ tsp. baking soda
- 1 cup boiling water
- 1 large egg yolk, lightly beaten

TOPPING

- 1½ cups all-purpose flour
- ¾ cup packed brown sugar
- ¾ tsp. baking soda
- Dash salt
- 6 Tbsp. cold butter, cubed

1. On a lightly floured surface, roll out dough to fit a 9-in. deep-dish pie plate. Trim and flute edge. Refrigerate at least 30 minutes.

2. Meanwhile, preheat oven to 425°. For filling, mix the brown sugar, molasses, egg, flour and baking soda. Gradually stir in boiling water; cool completely.

3. Line unpricked crust with a double thickness of foil. Fill with pie weights, dried beans or uncooked rice. Bake on a lower oven rack 15 minutes. Remove foil and pie weights; brush crust with egg yolk. Bake 5 minutes. Cool on a wire rack. Reduce oven setting to 350°.

4. In another bowl, whisk together first 4 topping ingredients. Cut in butter until crumbly. Add filling to crust; sprinkle with topping. Cover edge of pie with foil.

5. Bake until filling is set and golden brown, 45-50 minutes. Cool on a wire rack. Store in the refrigerator.

NOTE Let pie weights cool before storing. Beans and rice may be reused for pie weights, but not for cooking.

1 PIECE 540 cal., 22g fat (13g sat. fat), 99mg chol., 630mg sod., 82g carb. (49g sugars, 1g fiber), 6g pro.

DOUGH FOR SINGLE-CRUST PIE (9 IN.) Combine 1¼ cups all-purpose flour and ¼ tsp. salt; cut in ½ cup cold butter until crumbly. Gradually add 3-5 Tbsp. ice water, tossing with a fork until dough holds together when pressed. Cover and refrigerate 1 hour.

FUNNEL CAKES

When I was in high school, I made these funnel cakes for my family every Sunday after church. They are crisp and tender, just like the kind we always ate at the state fair.
—Susan Tingley

PREP: 15 MIN. • **COOK:** 5 MIN./BATCH
MAKES: 8 SERVINGS

- 2 cups 2% milk
- 3 large eggs, room temperature
- ¼ cup sugar
- 2 cups all-purpose flour
- 2 tsp. baking powder
- Oil for deep-fat frying
- Confectioners' sugar
- Optional toppings: Jam, chocolate sauce, caramel sauce or strawberry topping

1. In a large bowl, combine the milk, eggs and sugar. Combine flour and baking powder; beat into the egg mixture until smooth.

2. In a cast-iron or electric skillet, heat 2 in. oil to 375°. Cover the bottom of a funnel spout with your finger; ladle ½ cup batter into funnel. Holding the funnel several in. above the skillet, release your finger and move the funnel in a spiral motion until all the batter is released. Scrape funnel with a rubber spatula if needed.

3. Fry until golden brown, about 1 minute on each side. Drain on paper towels. Repeat with the remaining batter. Dust each cake with confectioners' sugar. Serve warm, with toppings if desired.

1 FUNNEL CAKE 300 cal., 15g fat (2g sat. fat), 84mg chol., 157mg sod., 33g carb. (10g sugars, 1g fiber), 8g pro.

FUN FOODS OF JERSEY SHORE

Funnel cake—crisp, lacy, and showered with confectioners' sugar—captures the boardwalk in every bite. For the full shore spirit, reach for salt water taffy and bright, lemony cups of Italian ice.

TENNESSEE
AIR-FRYER NASHVILLE
HOT CHICKEN, P. 44

DOWN SOUTH

The South's fields and farms lead to cooking with a little tang, a bit of heat and lots of satisfying richness. From fried chicken and green tomatoes to peach pudding and fruity cakes, the comfort here is worthy of second helpings.

SWEET TEA CONCENTRATE

Sweet iced tea is a southern classic, and this is a fabulous recipe for those tea lovers or for a party. The concentrate will make 20 servings.
—Natalie Bremson

PREP: 30 MIN. + COOLING
MAKES: 20 SERVINGS (5 CUPS CONCENTRATE)

- 2 medium lemons
- 4 cups sugar
- 4 cups water
- 1½ cups English breakfast tea leaves or 20 black tea bags

EACH SERVING

- 1 cup cold water
- Ice cubes

1. Using a vegetable peeler or a sharp paring knife, peel the lemon lengthwise into strips, peeling only the zest; reserve. Squeeze fruit, reserving ⅓ cup juice; save remaining juice for another use.
2. In a large saucepan, combine sugar and water. Bring to a boil over medium heat. Reduce heat; simmer, uncovered, until sugar is dissolved, 3-5 minutes, stirring occasionally. Remove from the heat; add tea leaves and lemon zest strips. Cover and steep for 15 minutes. Strain tea, discarding tea leaves and lemon zest; stir in reserved lemon juice. Cool to room temperature.
3. Transfer to a container with a tight-fitting lid. Store in the refrigerator for up to 2 weeks.
4. To prepare tea: In a tall glass, combine 1 cup cold water with ¼ cup concentrate; add ice.
¼ CUP CONCENTRATE 165 cal., 0 fat (0 sat. fat), 0 chol., 27mg sod., 43g carb. (40g sugars, 0 fiber), 0 pro.

MINI HOT BROWNS

Here's my take on Louisville's famous Hot Brown sandwich. Guests quickly line up for juicy turkey slices and crispy bacon piled on toasted rye bread and topped with a rich cheese sauce.
—Annette Grahl

TAKES: 30 MIN. • **MAKES:** 1½ DOZEN

- 1 tsp. chicken bouillon granules
- ¼ cup boiling water
- 3 Tbsp. butter
- 2 Tbsp. all-purpose flour
- ¾ cup half-and-half cream
- 1 cup shredded Swiss cheese
- 18 slices snack rye bread
- 6 oz. sliced deli turkey
- 1 small onion, thinly sliced and separated into rings
- 5 bacon strips, cooked and crumbled
- 2 Tbsp. minced fresh parsley

1. Preheat oven to 350°. Dissolve bouillon in water.
2. In a small saucepan, melt butter over medium heat. Stir in flour until smooth; add cream and bouillon. Bring to a boil; cook and stir until thickened, 1-2 minutes. Stir in the cheese until melted. Remove from the heat.
3. Place bread on 2 baking sheets. Layer each slice with turkey, onion and cheese mixture. Bake until heated through, 10-12 minutes. (Or preheat broiler and broil until edges of bread are crisp and sauce is bubbly, 3-5 minutes.) Sprinkle with bacon and parsley.

1 APPETIZER 98 cal., 6g fat (3g sat. fat), 21mg chol., 246mg sod., 5g carb. (1g sugars, 1g fiber), 5g pro.

MINT JULEP

It'll be hats off to you if you serve this classic cocktail at your next Kentucky Derby soiree. The subtly sweet sipper is an absolute must-have. Oh, and our nonalcoholic version hits the spot too!
—Taste of Home *Test Kitchen*

PREP: 30 MIN. + CHILLING
MAKES: 10 SERVINGS (2½ CUPS SYRUP)

MINT SYRUP

- 2 cups sugar
- 2 cups water
- 2 cups loosely packed chopped fresh mint

EACH SERVING

- ½ to ¾ cup crushed ice
- ½ to 1 oz. bourbon
- Mint sprig

1. For syrup, combine sugar, water and chopped mint in a large saucepan. Bring to a boil over medium heat; cook until sugar is dissolved, stirring occasionally. Remove from the heat; cool to room temperature.
2. Line a mesh strainer with a double layer of cheesecloth or a coffee filter. Strain syrup; discard mint. Cover and refrigerate syrup for at least 2 hours or until chilled.
3. For each serving, place ice in a metal julep cup or rocks glass. Pour 2-4 Tbsp. mint syrup and bourbon into the glass; stir until mixture is well chilled. Garnish with a mint sprig.

⅓ CUP 197 cal., 0 fat (0 sat. fat), 0 chol., 6mg sod., 42g carb. (39g sugars, 1g fiber), 1g pro.

MOCK MINT JULEP Prepare syrup as directed. After straining, add ½ cup lemon juice. Chill. For each serving, combine ½ cup club soda and ¼ cup mint syrup in a glass filled with crushed ice. Garnish with mint.

PULLED PORK NACHOS

I count on my slow cooker to do the honors when I have a house full of summer guests. Teenagers especially love DIY nachos. Try cola, ginger ale or lemon-lime soda as an alternative if you're not into root beer.
—James Schend

PREP: 20 MIN. • **COOK:** 8 HOURS
MAKES: 12 SERVINGS

- 1 boneless pork shoulder butt roast (3 to 4 lbs.)
- 1 can (12 oz.) root beer or cola
- 12 cups tortilla chips
- 2 cups shredded cheddar cheese
- 2 medium tomatoes, chopped
- Optional: Pico de gallo, chopped green onions and sliced jalapeno peppers

1. In a 4- or 5-qt. slow cooker, combine pork roast and root beer. Cook, covered, on low 8-9 hours or until meat is tender.
2. Remove roast; cool slightly. When cool enough to handle, shred meat with 2 forks. Return to slow cooker; keep warm.
3. To serve, drain pork. Layer tortilla chips with pork, cheese, tomatoes and optional toppings as desired. Serve immediately.

1 SERVING 391 cal., 23g fat (8g sat. fat), 86mg chol., 287mg sod., 20g carb. (4g sugars, 1g fiber), 25g pro.

MEMPHIS-STYLE BBQ RIBS

A friend of mine who loves barbecue gave me her recipe for ribs. I use just enough of the spice mixture to rub them before baking, and then sprinkle on the rest later.
—Jennifer Ross

PREP: 20 MIN. • **BAKE:** 3½ HOURS
MAKES: 6 SERVINGS

- ¼ cup packed brown sugar
- ¼ cup paprika
- 2 Tbsp. kosher salt
- 2 Tbsp. onion powder
- 2 Tbsp. garlic powder
- 2 Tbsp. coarsely ground pepper
- 3 racks (1½ to 2 lbs. each) pork baby back ribs
- Barbecue sauce, optional

1. Preheat oven to 350°. In a small bowl, mix the first 6 ingredients; rub ¾ cup over ribs. Wrap rib racks in large pieces of heavy-duty foil; seal tightly. Place in a 15x10x1-in. baking pan. Bake 1½ hours. Reduce oven setting to 250°. Bake until tender, about 1½ hours longer.
2. Carefully remove ribs from foil; return to baking pan. Sprinkle ribs with remaining spice mixture. Bake 30 minutes longer or until lightly browned, brushing with barbecue sauce, if desired.

1 SERVING 497 cal., 32g fat (11g sat. fat), 122mg chol., 2066mg sod., 17g carb. (10g sugars, 3g fiber), 35g pro.

FRIED CHICKEN

For our family, it's not a picnic unless there's fried chicken! Chicken, deviled eggs and potato salad are all musts for a picnic as far as my husband is concerned. This is a golden oldie recipe for me—I've used it many times through the years.
—Edna Hoffman

PREP: 30 MIN. + MARINATING
COOK: 40 MIN.
MAKES: 6 SERVINGS

- 1 broiler/fryer chicken (3 lbs.), cut up
- ¾ to 1 cup buttermilk

COATING

- 1½ to 2 cups all-purpose flour
- 1½ tsp. salt
- ½ tsp. pepper
- ½ tsp. garlic powder
- ½ tsp. onion powder
- 1 Tbsp. paprika
- ¼ tsp. ground sage
- ¼ tsp. ground thyme
- ¼ cayenne pepper, optional
- ⅛ tsp. baking powder
- Oil for frying

1. Pat chicken pieces with paper towels; place in large shallow dish. Pour buttermilk over chicken; cover and refrigerate at least 1 hour or overnight.

2. Combine coating ingredients in a shallow dish. Add chicken pieces, 1 at a time, and turn to coat. Lay coated pieces on waxed paper for 15 minutes to allow coating to dry (this will help coating cling during frying).

3. In a Dutch oven or deep skillet, heat ½ in. oil over medium heat to 350°. Fry chicken in batches, uncovered, turning occasionally, until coating is dark golden brown and meat is no longer pink, 7-8 minutes per side. Drain on paper towels; if desired, sprinkle with additional salt and pepper.

5 OZ. COOKED CHICKEN 623 cal., 40g fat (7g sat. fat), 106mg chol., 748mg sod., 26g carb. (2g sugars, 1g fiber), 38g pro.

READER REVIEW

"I added a bit of Cajun seasoning to it. Add a batch of fresh buttermilk biscuits—now that is cooking!"
—RUBYD00008, TASTEOFHOME.COM

OLD BAY
SEASONING
CRABS
SHRIMP
For Seafood, Poultry, Salads, Meats

LOWCOUNTRY BOIL

Ideal for camping and relaxing trips to the beach, this crowd-pleasing recipe makes an appetizing presentation of perfectly seasoned meats, veggies and seafood.
—Mageswari Elagupillai, Victorville, CA

PREP: 20 MIN. • **COOK:** 40 MIN.
MAKES: 4 SERVINGS

- 2 qt. water
- 1 bottle (12 oz.) beer
- 2 Tbsp. seafood seasoning
- 1½ tsp. salt
- 4 medium red potatoes, cut into wedges
- 1 medium sweet onion, cut into wedges
- 4 medium ears sweet corn, cut in half
- ⅓ lb. smoked chorizo or kielbasa, cut into 1-in. slices
- 3 Tbsp. olive oil
- 6 large garlic cloves, minced
- 1 Tbsp. ground cumin
- 1 Tbsp. minced fresh cilantro
- ½ tsp. paprika
- ½ tsp. pepper
- 1 lb. uncooked shrimp (26-30 per lb.), peeled and deveined
- 1 lb. uncooked snow crab legs
- Optional: Seafood cocktail sauce, lemon wedges and melted butter

1. In a Dutch oven, combine water, beer, seafood seasoning and salt; add potatoes and onion. Bring to a boil. Reduce heat and simmer, uncovered, 10 minutes. Add corn and chorizo; simmer until potatoes and corn are tender, 10-12 minutes longer.

2. Meanwhile, in a small skillet, heat oil. Add garlic, cumin, cilantro, paprika and pepper. Cook and stir over medium heat for 1 minute.

3. Stir shrimp, crab legs and garlic mixture into the Dutch oven; cook until shrimp and crab turn pink, 4-6 minutes. Drain; transfer seafood mixture to a large serving bowl. Serve with condiments of your choice.

1 SERVING 500 cal., 20g fat (5g sat. fat), 212mg chol., 1318mg sod., 41g carb. (6g sugars, 5g fiber), 40g pro.

LOVE THAT LOWCOUNTRY

The one-pot feast of shrimp, sausage and veggies is sometimes called Frogmore Stew or Beaufort Stew after the coastal South Carolina towns where this dish originated. Purists debate the add-ins—crab or no crab, onions or no onions, beer or not—but the spirit is always simple and social. Scale the pot to your crew, drain it onto a newspaper-lined table, and have at it, seated elbow to elbow.

AIR-FRYER NASHVILLE HOT CHICKEN

I am from Tennessee and we love Nashville and chicken, so I thought why not make some Nashville Hot Chicken in the air fryer?
—April H. Lane

PREP: 20 MIN. + MARINATING
COOK: 15 MIN./BATCH
MAKES: 6 SERVINGS

- 2 lbs. chicken tenderloins
- 1½ tsp. salt
- 2 tsp. pepper
- 2 Tbsp. dill pickle juice
- 2 Tbsp. Louisiana-style hot sauce, divided
- 3 cups all-purpose flour
- 3 large eggs
- 1½ cups buttermilk
- ¾ cup olive oil
- 4 Tbsp. cayenne pepper
- 2 Tbsp. packed brown sugar
- 1 tsp. chili powder
- 1 tsp. garlic powder
- 1 tsp. paprika
- Optional: Dill pickle slices and white bread

1. Preheat air fryer to 400°. In a shallow bowl, combine chicken, salt, pepper, pickle juice and 1 Tbsp. hot sauce. Cover; refrigerate for at least 2 hours. To another shallow bowl, add flour. Whisk together eggs, buttermilk and remaining 1 Tbsp. hot sauce. Dip chicken in flour, then in buttermilk mixture, and then back in flour, patting to help it adhere.

2. In batches, arrange chicken in a single layer in greased air-fryer basket; spritz with cooking spray. Cook until golden brown and chicken is no longer pink, 7-8 minutes on each side. To make spicy sauce, combine oil and remaining ingredients. Immediately pour over chicken. If desired, serve with pickles and white bread.

1 SERVING 531 cal., 31g fat (5g sat. fat), 137mg chol., 960mg sod., 25g carb. (6g sugars, 2g fiber), 41g pro.

SERVING SUGGESTION

Nashville Hot Chicken is traditionally served with white bread and pickles to help balance the spiciness. You can also enjoy it alongside cooling foods such as cottage cheese or ranch dressing, or with classic fried chicken sides like french fries or Tater Tots.

CAROLINA-STYLE VINEGAR BBQ CHICKEN

I live in Georgia, but I appreciate the tangy, sweet and slightly spicy taste of Carolina vinegar chicken. I make my version in the slow cooker. With the tempting aroma filling the house, your family is sure to be at the dinner table on time!
—Ramona Parris

PREP: 10 MIN. • **COOK:** 4 HOURS
MAKES: 6 SERVINGS

- 2 cups water
- 1 cup white vinegar
- ¼ cup sugar
- 1 Tbsp. reduced-sodium chicken base
- 1 tsp. crushed red pepper flakes
- ¾ tsp. salt
- 1½ lbs. boneless skinless chicken breasts
- 6 whole wheat hamburger buns, split, optional

1. In a small bowl, mix the first 6 ingredients. Place chicken in a 3-qt. slow cooker; add vinegar mixture. Cook, covered, on low 4-5 hours or until chicken is tender.
2. Remove chicken; cool slightly. Reserve 1 cup cooking juices; discard remaining juices. Shred chicken with 2 forks. Return meat and reserved cooking juices to slow cooker; heat through. If desired, serve chicken mixture on buns.
NOTE Look for chicken base near the broth and bouillon.
½ CUP 134 cal., 3g fat (1g sat. fat), 63mg chol., 228mg sod., 3g carb. (3g sugars, 0 fiber), 23g pro.

FRIED GREEN TOMATOES

My grandmother came up with her own version of fried green tomatoes years ago. Our family loves them. It's a traditional taste of the South that anyone anywhere can enjoy!
—Melanie Chism

PREP: 10 MIN. + STANDING
COOK: 10 MIN.
MAKES: 8 SERVINGS

- 4 medium green tomatoes
- 1 tsp. salt
- ¼ tsp. lemon-pepper seasoning
- ¾ cup cornmeal
- ½ cup vegetable oil

Slice tomatoes ¼ in. thick. Sprinkle both sides with salt and lemon-pepper seasoning. Let stand 20-25 minutes. Coat with cornmeal. In a large skillet, heat oil over medium heat. Fry tomatoes until tender and golden brown, 3-4 minutes on each side. Drain on paper towels. Serve immediately.
2 PIECES 166 cal., 11g fat (1g sat. fat), 0 chol., 317mg sod., 16g carb. (4g sugars, 2g fiber), 2g pro.

ORIGIN STORY

Most "green tomatoes" are simply unripened red ones—picked firm for a tart snap or at season's end to save the last fruits before frost. Popularized at Alabama's Irondale Cafe, the Southern classic shines with tangy remoulade, buttermilk ranch, spicy mayo, hot honey or pimiento-cheese spread.

ROLLED BUTTERMILK BISCUITS

I scribbled down this recipe when our family visited The Farmers' Museum in Cooperstown, New York, more than 25 years ago. I must have gotten it right, because these biscuits turn out great every time.
—*Patricia Kile*

PREP: 20 MIN. • **BAKE:** 15 MIN.
MAKES: 8 BISCUITS

- 2 cups all-purpose flour
- 3 tsp. baking powder
- ½ tsp. baking soda
- ¼ tsp. salt
- 3 Tbsp. cold butter
- ¾ to 1 cup buttermilk
- 1 Tbsp. fat-free milk

1. Preheat oven to 450°. In a large bowl, combine the flour, baking powder, baking soda and salt; cut in butter until mixture resembles coarse crumbs. Stir in enough buttermilk just to moisten dough.
2. Turn onto a lightly floured surface; knead 3-4 times. Pat or roll to ¾-in. thickness. Cut with a floured 2½-in. biscuit cutter. Place in a large ungreased cast-iron or other ovenproof skillet.
3. Brush with milk. Bake until golden brown, 12-15 minutes.

1 BISCUIT 162 cal., 5g fat (3g sat. fat), 12mg chol., 412mg sod., 25g carb. (1g sugars, 1g fiber), 4g pro.

SAUSAGE GRAVY

This is an old southern recipe that I've adapted. It's the kind of hearty breakfast that will warm you right up.
—*Sue Baker*

TAKES: 15 MIN.
MAKES: 2 SERVINGS

- ¼ lb. bulk pork sausage
- 2 Tbsp. butter
- 2 to 3 Tbsp. all-purpose flour
- ¼ tsp. salt
- ⅛ tsp. pepper
- 1¼ to 1⅓ cups whole milk
- Warm biscuits

In a small skillet, cook sausage over medium heat until no longer pink, 3-5 minutes, breaking it up into crumbles; drain. Add butter and heat until melted. Add the flour, salt and pepper; cook and stir until blended. Gradually add the milk, stirring constantly. Bring to a boil; cook and stir until thickened, about 2 minutes. Serve with biscuits.

¾ CUP 337 cal., 27g fat (14g sat. fat), 72mg chol., 718mg sod., 14g carb. (8g sugars, 0 fiber), 10g pro.

ROUX YOUR OWN WAY

Many traditionalists prefer their roux using sausage fat only—not butter. To prepare it this way, don't drain the fat from the sausage; add butter only if you need it to equal 2 to 3 Tbsp. of total fat (you will then add 2 to 3 Tbsp. of flour to create the roux). Be careful not to overbrown.

BLACK-EYED PEAS WITH COLLARD GREENS

This dish has special meaning on New Year's Day, when Southerners eat greens for future wealth and black-eyed peas for prosperity.
—*Athena Russell*

TAKES: 25 MIN.
MAKES: 6 SERVINGS

- 2 Tbsp. olive oil
- 1 garlic clove, minced
- 8 cups chopped collard greens
- ½ tsp. salt
- ¼ tsp. cayenne pepper
- 2 cans (15½ oz. each) black-eyed peas, rinsed and drained
- 4 plum tomatoes, seeded and chopped
- ¼ cup lemon juice
- 2 Tbsp. grated Parmesan cheese

In a Dutch oven, heat oil over medium heat. Add garlic; cook and stir 1 minute. Add collard greens, salt and cayenne; cook and stir 6-8 minutes or until greens are tender. Add peas, tomatoes and lemon juice; heat through. Sprinkle servings with cheese.

¾ CUP 177 cal., 5g fat (1g sat. fat), 1mg chol., 412mg sod., 24g carb. (3g sugars, 6g fiber), 9g pro.

INGREDIENT SPOTLIGHT

Black-eyed peas came to the U.S. with enslaved West Africans in the 1600s. In their cultures, peas represented protection and good luck. Some families trace the New Year's custom to January 1, 1863, when the Emancipation Proclamation took effect. The peas also symbolize coins and the collard greens, paper bills—making this dish a double dose of good fortune in the new year.

AMBROSIA SALAD

Because it's so easy to prepare, this tropical medley is great as a last-minute menu addition. Plus, it requires just five ingredients.
—Judi Bringegar

PREP: 10 MIN. + CHILLING
MAKES: 6 SERVINGS

- 1 can (15 oz.) mandarin oranges, drained
- 1 can (8 oz.) pineapple tidbits, drained
- 1 cup miniature marshmallows
- 1 cup sweetened shredded coconut
- 1 cup sour cream

In a large bowl, combine oranges, pineapple, marshmallows and coconut. Add sour cream and toss to mix. Cover and refrigerate for several hours.

⅔ CUP 247 cal., 14g fat (10g sat. fat), 28mg chol., 67mg sod., 32g carb. (29g sugars, 1g fiber), 2g pro.

READER REVIEW

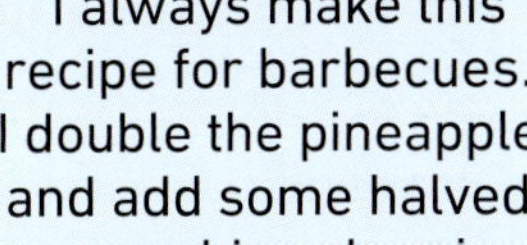

"I always make this recipe for barbecues. I double the pineapple and add some halved maraschino cherries for color."
—SCENT4U, TASTEOFHOME.COM

PIG PICKIN' CAKE

This is one of my favorite cakes. It's moist and light, yet so satisfying. I've been adapting it for years and now it's almost guilt free.
—Pam Sjolund

PREP: 15 MIN.
BAKE: 25 MIN. + CHILLING
MAKES: 15 SERVINGS

- 1 pkg. yellow cake mix (regular size)
- 1 can (11 oz.) mandarin oranges, undrained
- 4 large egg whites, room temperature
- ½ cup unsweetened applesauce

TOPPING

- 1 can (20 oz.) crushed pineapple, undrained
- 1 pkg. (1 oz.) sugar-free instant vanilla pudding mix
- 1 carton (8 oz.) reduced-fat whipped topping

1. In a large bowl, beat the cake mix, oranges, egg whites and applesauce on low speed for 2 minutes. Pour into a 13x9-in. baking dish coated with cooking spray.

2. Bake at 350° for 25-30 minutes or until a toothpick inserted in the center comes out clean. Cool on a wire rack.

3. In a bowl, combine the pineapple and pudding mix. Fold in whipped topping just until blended. Spread over cake. Refrigerate for at least 1 hour before serving.

1 PIECE 218 cal., 3g fat (2g sat. fat), 0 chol., 338mg sod., 47g carb. (27g sugars, 1g fiber), 2g pro.

LADY BALTIMORE CAKE

I first made this cake for my father's'birthday and now it is the only cake that he requests. The cake has complex flavors and is decidedly unique.
—*Cleo Gonske*

PREP: 30 MIN. + STANDING
BAKE: 20 MIN. + COOLING
MAKES: 16 SERVINGS

- 1⅔ cups raisins, chopped
- 8 dried figs, finely chopped
- ½ cup brandy

CAKE

- 2½ cups all-purpose flour
- 2 cups sugar
- 2 tsp. grated orange zest
- 1 tsp. baking powder
- ½ tsp. baking soda
- ⅛ tsp. salt
- 1⅓ cups buttermilk
- ½ cup butter, softened
- 1 tsp. vanilla extract
- 4 large egg whites, room temperature

FROSTING

- 2 cups butter, softened
- 6 cups confectioners' sugar, sifted
- 2 tsp. vanilla extract
- ¼ to ⅓ cup heavy whipping cream
- 1 cup finely chopped pecans, toasted

1. In a small bowl, combine raisins and figs. Add brandy and toss to combine. Let stand, covered, at room temperature until brandy is absorbed, about 2 hours, stirring occasionally.
2. Preheat oven to 350°. Line bottoms of 3 greased 8-in. round cake pans with parchment; grease the paper.
3. In a large bowl, mix flour, sugar, orange zest, baking powder, baking soda and salt until blended. Add buttermilk, butter and vanilla; beat on low speed 30 seconds or just until dry ingredients are moistened. Beat on medium for 2 minutes. Add egg whites; beat 2 minutes longer.
4. Transfer batter to prepared pans. Bake until a toothpick inserted in center comes out clean, 20-25 minutes. Cool in pans 10 minutes before removing to wire racks to cool completely.
5. For frosting, in a large bowl, cream butter until fluffy. Gradually beat in confectioners' sugar. Beat in vanilla and enough cream to reach desired consistency. For filling, remove 1 cup frosting to a small bowl; stir in pecans and raisin mixture.
6. Place 1 cake layer on a serving plate; spread with half the filling. Add another cake layer; top with remaining filling. Add remaining cake layer; spread remaining frosting over top and side of cake.

NOTES To substitute for each cup of buttermilk, use 1 Tbsp. white vinegar or lemon juice plus enough milk to measure 1 cup. Stir, then let stand 5 min. Or use 1 cup plain yogurt or 1¾ tsp. cream of tartar plus 1 cup milk. To toast nuts, bake in a shallow pan in a 350°; oven for 5-10 minutes or cook in a skillet over low heat until lightly browned, stirring occasionally.

1 PIECE 745 cal., 36g fat (20g sat. fat), 81mg chol., 373mg sod., 102g carb. (82g sugars, 2g fiber), 5g pro.

ORIGIN STORY

The beloved cake traces to the Lady Baltimore Tea Room in Charleston, South Carolina, around 1900. Its fame leapt after Owen Wister's 1903 novel *Lady Baltimore* rhapsodized a Charleston tea-room slice, cementing the Lowcountry claim to this airy fruit-and-pecan–filled classic.

TENNESSEE PEACH PUDDING

This out-of-this-world dessert is one of our favorite peach recipes. I was raised in Oklahoma, and we used Elberta peaches right off our trees when we made this outstanding cobbler.
—Virginia Crowell

PREP: 20 MIN. • **BAKE:** 40 MIN.
MAKES: 8 SERVINGS

- 1 cup all-purpose flour
- ½ cup sugar
- 2 tsp. baking powder
- ½ tsp. salt
- ½ tsp. ground cinnamon, optional
- ½ cup 2% milk
- 3 cups sliced peeled fresh or frozen peaches

TOPPING

- 1½ cups water
- ½ cup sugar
- ½ cup packed brown sugar
- 1 Tbsp. butter
- ¼ tsp. ground nutmeg
- Vanilla ice cream, optional

1. Preheat oven to 400°. Combine flour, sugar, baking powder, salt and, if desired, cinnamon. Stir in milk just until combined; fold in peaches. Spread into a greased 8-in. square baking dish.

2. For topping, combine water, sugars, butter and nutmeg in a large saucepan. Bring to a boil, stirring until sugars are dissolved. Pour over peach mixture. Bake until filling is bubbly and a toothpick inserted in topping comes out clean, 40-50 minutes. Serve warm or cold, with ice cream if desired.

1 SERVING 253 cal., 2g fat (1g sat. fat), 5mg chol., 269mg sod., 57g carb. (44g sugars, 1g fiber), 3g pro.

MISSISSIPPI
CATFISH &
HUSH PUPPIES,
P. 60

FLORIDA & GULF COAST

The cuisine of the Gulf states is shaped by shrimp boats, oyster beds, river deltas and Caribbean currents. From gumbo and crawfish to rum runners and Key lime pie, the specialties on this stretch of coast serve up sunshine with a sassy snap.

CRAWFISH BEIGNETS WITH CAJUN DIPPING SAUCE

Get a taste of the Deep South with these slightly spicy beignets. You won't be able to eat just one!
—Donna Lanclos

PREP: 20 MIN.
COOK: 5 MIN./BATCH
MAKES: ABOUT 2 DOZEN (¾ CUP SAUCE)

- 1 large egg, beaten
- 1 lb. chopped cooked crawfish tail meat or shrimp
- 4 green onions, chopped
- 1½ tsp. butter, melted
- ½ tsp. salt
- ½ tsp. cayenne pepper
- ⅓ cup bread flour
- Oil for deep-fat frying
- ¾ cup mayonnaise
- ½ cup ketchup
- ¼ tsp. prepared horseradish, optional
- ¼ tsp. hot pepper sauce

1. In a large bowl, combine the egg, crawfish, green onions, butter, salt and cayenne. Stir in the flour until blended.
2. In an electric skillet or deep fryer, heat 1 in. oil to 375°. Drop batter by tablespoonfuls, a few at a time, into hot oil. Fry until golden brown on both sides. Drain on paper towels.
3. In a small bowl, combine the mayonnaise, ketchup, horseradish if desired, and pepper sauce. Serve with beignets.

1 BEIGNET WITH 1½ TSP. SAUCE 101 cal., 8g fat (1g sat. fat), 35mg chol., 171mg sod., 3g carb. (1g sugars, 0 fiber), 4g pro.

FRIED DILL PICKLES

You may be surprised when you see how easy it is to make a batch of these fried pickles. They'll get snatched up in a flash!
—Eloise Maynor

TAKES: 20 MIN. • **MAKES:** 3½ CUPS

- 1 jar (32 oz.) whole dill pickles
- 1 cup buttermilk
- 2 Tbsp. Louisiana-style hot sauce
- 1 cup all-purpose flour
- 1 cup cornmeal
- 2 Tbsp. garlic salt
- 2 Tbsp. paprika
- 1 Tbsp. cayenne pepper
- 1 tsp. pepper
- Oil for deep-fat frying
- Ranch salad dressing, optional

1. Drain pickles, discarding liquid. Cut pickles into ½-in.-thick slices. Drain on paper towels; blot with additional paper towels until dry.
2. In a shallow bowl, mix buttermilk and hot sauce. In another shallow bowl, mix flour, cornmeal, garlic salt, paprika, cayenne pepper and pepper. Dip pickles in buttermilk mixture, then in flour mixture. In a Dutch oven, heat 1 in. of oil to 375°. Working in batches, fry pickles 2-3 minutes on each side or until golden brown. Drain on paper towels. Serve immediately with ranch dressing if desired.

¼ CUP 94 cal., 5g fat (0 sat. fat), 0 chol., 1237mg sod., 9g carb. (1g sugars, 1g fiber), 1g pro.

RUM RUNNER

With its ambrosial blend of fruity, sugary island flavors, a rum runner will whisk you off to the tropics from the very first sip. Thanks to all its fruity flavors, this strong cocktail goes down deceptively easy.
—Shawn Barto

TAKES: 10 MIN. • **MAKES:** 1 SERVING

Ice cubes
1 oz. light rum
1 oz. dark rum
1 oz. blackberry liqueur
1 oz. banana liqueur
1 oz. orange juice
1 oz. pineapple juice
Splash grenadine syrup
Optional garnishes: Maraschino cherry, orange slice or pineapple wedge

Fill a shaker three-fourths full with ice. Add the rums, liqueurs, juices and grenadine. Cover and shake for 15-20 seconds or until condensation forms on outside of shaker. Strain into a chilled cocktail glass with ice. Garnish as desired.

1 SERVING 365 cal., 0 fat (0 sat. fat), 0 chol., 1mg sod., 29g carb. (28g sugars, 0 fiber), 0 pro.

ORIGIN STORY

Born in the Florida Keys at the Holiday Isle Tiki Bar, the Rum Runner was mixed to use up extra bottles before new stock arrived. Its name nods to Prohibition smugglers who ferried Bahamian rum into the area by boat. Fruity, boozy, and beachy, it's built for unwinding on island time.

OYSTERS ROCKEFELLER

My husband and I delight guests with this classic dish that originated in New Orleans. It's deliciously simple!
—Beth Walton

PREP: 1¼ HOURS • **BAKE:** 10 MIN.
MAKES: 3 DOZEN

- 1 medium onion, finely chopped
- ½ cup butter, cubed
- 1 pkg. (9 oz.) fresh spinach, torn
- 1 cup grated Romano cheese
- 1 Tbsp. lemon juice
- ⅛ tsp. pepper
- 2 lbs. kosher salt
- 3 dozen fresh oysters in the shell, washed

1. In a large skillet, saute onion in butter until tender. Add spinach; cook and stir until wilted. Remove from the heat; stir in cheese, lemon juice and pepper.

2. Spread the kosher salt into 2 ungreased 15x10x1-in. baking pans. Shuck oysters, reserving oyster and its liquid in bottom shell. Lightly press oyster shells down into the salt, using salt to keep the oysters level. Top each with 2½ tsp. spinach mixture.

3. Bake, uncovered, at 450° until oysters are plump, 6-8 minutes. Serve immediately.

1 OYSTER 79 cal., 5g fat (3g sat. fat), 35mg chol., 133mg sod., 3g carb. (0 sugars, 0 fiber), 6g pro.

READER REVIEW

"Hardest part is shucking the oysters. My seafood store did that for me, so the only work was making the topping and broiling them. I used a muffin pan instead of rock salt to hold the oysters in place; it worked great. Huge hit with my guests. Enormous crowd pleaser and super easy."
—LYNNETHLOHSE, TASTEOFHOME.COM

HEARTY RED BEANS & RICE

I take this dish to many potlucks and never fail to bring home an empty pot. I learned about the mouthwatering combination of meats, beans and seasonings while working for the Navy in New Orleans. If you want to get a head start, cover the beans with water and let them soak overnight. Drain them the next day and continue with the recipe as directed.
—Kathy Jacques

PREP: 15 MIN. + SOAKING
COOK: 2 HOURS
MAKES: 10 SERVINGS

- 1 lb. dried kidney beans
- 2 tsp. garlic salt
- 1 tsp. Worcestershire sauce
- ¼ tsp. hot pepper sauce
- 1 qt. water
- ½ lb. fully cooked ham, diced
- ½ lb. fully cooked smoked sausage, diced
- 1 cup chopped onion
- ½ cup chopped celery
- 3 garlic cloves, minced
- 1 can (8 oz.) tomato sauce
- 2 bay leaves
- ¼ cup minced fresh parsley
- ½ tsp. salt
- ½ tsp. pepper
- Hot cooked rice

1. Place beans in a Dutch oven; add enough water to cover by 2 in. Bring to a boil; boil for 2 minutes. Remove from the heat; cover and let stand for 1-4 hours or until softened.
2. Drain beans, discarding liquid. Add the garlic salt, Worcestershire sauce, hot pepper sauce and water; bring to a boil. Reduce heat; cover and simmer for 1½ hours.
3. Meanwhile, in a large skillet, saute ham and sausage until lightly browned. Remove with a slotted spoon to bean mixture. Saute onion and celery in drippings until tender. Add garlic; cook 1 minute longer. Add to bean mixture. Stir in tomato sauce and bay leaves. Cover and simmer for 30 minutes or until beans are tender.
4. Discard bay leaves. Remove 2 cups bean mixture to a small bowl; mash and return to the pot. Stir in the parsley, salt and pepper. Serve over rice.

1 CUP 276 cal., 9g fat (3g sat. fat), 27mg chol., 1149mg sod., 32g carb. (4g sugars, 8g fiber), 18g pro.

MONDAY MEANS RED BEANS

Slow-simmered red beans is a Monday classic in New Orleans. The pot simmers all day—usually with a leftover ham bone from Sunday's dinner—while household chores are completed. Serve the stewed beans over steamed rice with hot sauce for a comforting start to the week.

SHRIMP BOIL

This shrimp boil is meant for a crowd. The spicy sausage, soft potatoes and tender corn are packed with flavor. Add a squeeze of lemon for some brightness.
—Taste of Home *Test Kitchen*

PREP: 10 MIN. • **COOK:** 35 MIN.
MAKES: 8 SERVINGS

- 4 qt. water
- 1 large onion, cut into 6 wedges
- 1 whole garlic bulb, halved horizontally
- ½ cup seafood seasoning
- 6 medium red potatoes, quartered
- 4 medium ears sweet corn, cut into thirds
- ¾ lb. fully cooked andouille sausage links, cut into 1-in. pieces
- 2 lbs. uncooked shell-on shrimp (26-30 per lb.)
- ½ cup butter, melted
- Lemon wedges

1. In a stockpot, combine water, onion, garlic and seafood seasoning; bring to a boil. Add the potatoes; cook, uncovered, 10 minutes. Add corn and sausage; return to a boil. Reduce the heat; simmer, uncovered, until potatoes are tender, 8-10 minutes. Add the shrimp; cook until shrimp turn pink, 2-3 minutes longer.

2. Drain; transfer to a large serving platter. Drizzle with butter. Serve with lemon wedges and, if desired, additional seafood seasoning.

1 SERVING 410 cal., 22g fat (11g sat. fat), 224mg chol., 813mg sod., 25g carb. (4g sugars, 3g fiber), 30g pro.

CRAWFISH FETTUCCINE

I have lived in the close-knit Gulf community all my life and enjoy cooking Cajun dishes, especially those with seafood. Along with a green salad and garlic bread, this dish is great for family gatherings. The recipe can easily be doubled to serve a larger group, and if you'd like it less spicy, remove the seeds from the jalapeno before chopping it.
—Carolyn Lejeune

PREP: 30 MIN. • **COOK:** 30 MIN.
MAKES: 8 SERVINGS

- 1 large onion, chopped
- 1 medium sweet red pepper, chopped
- 2/3 cup sliced green onions
- 1 celery rib, chopped
- 1¼ cups butter, cubed
- 1 garlic clove, minced
- ¼ cup all-purpose flour
- 8 oz. Velveeta, cubed
- 1 cup half-and-half cream
- 1 Tbsp. chopped jalapeno pepper
- ½ tsp. salt
- 8 oz. uncooked fettuccine
- 1½ lbs. frozen cooked crawfish tails, thawed or cooked medium shrimp, peeled and deveined

1. In a Dutch oven or large skillet, saute the onion, red pepper, green onions and celery in butter until vegetables are crisp-tender, about 5 minutes. Add garlic; cook 1 minute longer. Stir in flour until blended; cook and stir 2 minutes. Add the cheese, cream, jalapeno and salt; cook and stir until the mixture is thickened and cheese is melted, about 10 minutes.

2. Meanwhile, cook fettuccine according to package directions; drain. Stir fettuccine and crawfish into the vegetable mixture. Cook, uncovered, over medium heat until heated through, about 10 minutes, stirring occasionally.

NOTE Wear disposable gloves when cutting hot peppers; the oils can burn skin. Avoid touching your face.

1 CUP 590 cal., 41g fat (25g sat. fat), 236mg chol., 853mg sod., 30g carb. (5g sugars, 2g fiber), 26g pro.

CATFISH & HUSH PUPPIES

Catfish and hush puppies are a match made in Mississippi. This southern dish combines two delicious fried foods on one comforting plate.
—*Margaret Knoebel*

PREP: 25 MIN. + STANDING.
COOK: 25 MIN.
MAKES: 6 SERVINGS

- 1 large egg white
- 1 cup whole milk
- 1 cup cornmeal
- 1 tsp. seafood seasoning
- 6 catfish fillets (6 oz. each)
- Oil for deep-fat frying

HUSH PUPPIES

- 1 cup cornmeal
- 1 cup self-rising flour
- 1½ tsp. baking powder
- ½ tsp. salt
- ¼ cup chopped green onions
- ¼ cup sugar
- 1 large egg, room temperature
- 1 cup buttermilk
- Optional: Lemon wedges and tartar sauce

1. In a shallow bowl, beat the egg white until foamy; add milk and mix well. In another shallow bowl, combine the cornmeal and seafood seasoning. Dip fillets in the milk mixture, then coat with cornmeal mixture.

2. In an electric skillet or deep fryer, heat 2-3 in. oil; fry the fish over medium-high heat for 3-4 minutes on each side or until it flakes easily with a fork.

3. For the hush puppies, in a large bowl, combine first 6 ingredients. Add egg and buttermilk; stir just until moistened. Let stand at room temperature for 30 minutes. Do not stir again.

4. In the same electric skillet or deep fryer, drop batter by rounded tablespoonfuls into the hot oil, a few at a time. Fry until golden brown, about 1½ minutes on each side. Drain on paper towels. If desired, serve catfish and hush puppies with and lemon wedges and tartar sauce.

1 SERVING 490 cal., 14g fat (3g sat. fat), 127mg chol., 859mg sod., 54g carb. (12g sugars, 2g fiber), 33g pro.

DEEP SOUTH FISH FRY

All along the Gulf Coast—from Gulfport, Mississippi, and west to the Delta in New Orleans—fried catfish with hush puppies is year-round comfort food. Mississippi's thriving catfish farms keep the platters overflowing, typically with coleslaw and french fries on the side.

SHRIMP GUMBO

A crisp green salad and crusty French bread complete this fabulous meal. I always have hot sauce available when I serve this, and have found that the instant microwave rice packages make the process a little easier.
—Jo Ann Graham

PREP: 30 MIN. • **COOK:** 1 HOUR
MAKES: 11 SERVINGS (2¾ QT.)

- ¼ cup all-purpose flour
- ¼ cup canola oil
- 3 celery ribs, chopped
- 1 medium green pepper, chopped
- 1 medium onion, chopped
- 4 cups chicken broth
- 3 garlic cloves, minced
- 1 tsp. salt
- 1 tsp. pepper
- ½ tsp. cayenne pepper
- 2 lbs. uncooked shrimp (26-30 per lb.), peeled and deveined
- 1 pkg. (16 oz.) frozen sliced okra
- 4 green onions, sliced
- 1 medium tomato, chopped
- 1½ tsp. gumbo file powder
- Hot cooked rice

1. In a Dutch oven over medium heat, cook and stir flour and oil until caramel-colored, stirring occasionally, about 12 minutes (do not burn). Add the celery, green pepper and onion; cook and stir until tender, 5-6 minutes. Stir in the broth, garlic, salt, pepper and cayenne; bring to a boil. Reduce the heat; cover and simmer for 30 minutes.

2. Stir in the shrimp, okra, green onions and tomato. Return to a boil. Reduce heat; cover and simmer until the shrimp turn pink, about 10 minutes. Stir in file powder. Serve with rice.

NOTE Gumbo file powder, used to thicken and flavor Creole recipes, is available in spice shops. If you don't want to use gumbo file powder, combine 2 Tbsp. each cornstarch and cold water until smooth. Gradually stir into gumbo. Bring to a boil; cook and stir for 2 minutes or until thickened.

1 CUP 159 cal., 7g fat (1g sat. fat), 102mg chol., 681mg sod., 9g carb. (3g sugars, 2g fiber), 15g pro.

CAJUN MIREPOIX

Celery, onion and green pepper is a classic Creole combination called holy trinity or Cajun mirepoix. Standard mirepoix, a base for many American soups and sauces, uses carrot instead of green pepper.

SLOW-COOKER CUBANO SANDWICHES

This recipe came about when I didn't have pepperoncini for my Italian pork recipe, so I used pickles instead. It reminded me of a Cuban sandwich, so I added some ham and Swiss to complete the dish. Instead of adding cheese to the slow cooker, you can use it to top the sandwiches and place them under the broiler.
—Kristie Schley

PREP: 15 MIN. • **COOK:** 6½ HOURS
MAKES: 8 SERVINGS

- 2 lbs. pork tenderloin
- 7 Tbsp. stone-ground mustard, divided
- 1 tsp. pepper, freshly ground
- 1 lb. fully cooked boneless ham steak, cut into ½-in. cubes
- 1 jar (16 oz.) whole baby dill pickles, undrained, sliced thick
- 2 cups shredded Swiss cheese
- 8 submarine buns, split

1. Rub pork with 3 Tbsp. mustard, season with pepper and place in a 5- or 6-qt. slow cooker. Add ham and pickles, including pickle juice. Cover and cook on low 6 hours or until tender, turning halfway through.
2. Shred pork with 2 forks. Sprinkle cheese over meat mixture; cover and cook until cheese melts, about 30 minutes.
3. When ready to serve, slice rolls and toast lightly in a toaster oven or broiler. Spread remaining 4 Tbsp. mustard evenly over both sides. Using a slotted spoon, top rolls with meat mixture. Serve immediately.
1 SANDWICH 526 cal., 20g fat (8g sat. fat), 118mg chol., 1941mg sod., 36g carb. (4g sugars, 3g fiber), 48g pro.

FIRECRACKER POTATO SALAD

I could eat potato salad all the time. A little spice is nice, so I use cayenne and paprika in this grilled salad.
—Ashley Armstrong

PREP: 20 MIN.
GRILL: 20 MIN. + CHILLING
MAKES: 16 SERVINGS

- 3 lbs. small red potatoes (about 30), quartered
- 2 Tbsp. olive oil
- 1 tsp. salt
- ½ tsp. pepper

DRESSING
- 1½ cups mayonnaise
- ½ cup finely chopped onion
- ¼ cup Dijon mustard
- 2 Tbsp. sweet pickle relish
- ½ tsp. paprika
- ¼ tsp. cayenne pepper

SALAD
- 6 hard-boiled large eggs, chopped
- 2 celery ribs, finely chopped
- Minced fresh chives, optional

1. Toss potatoes with oil, salt and pepper; place in a grill wok or basket. Grill, covered, over medium heat 20-25 minutes or until potatoes are tender, stirring occasionally. Transfer potatoes to a large bowl; cool slightly.
2. In a small bowl, mix dressing ingredients. Add dressing, eggs and celery to potatoes; toss to combine. Refrigerate, covered, 1-2 hours or until cold. If desired, sprinkle with chives.
NOTE If you do not have a grill wok or basket, use a large disposable foil pan and poke holes in the bottom of the pan.
1 CUP 265 cal., 20g fat (3g sat. fat), 77mg chol., 398mg sod., 16g carb. (2g sugars, 2g fiber), 4g pro.

SLOW-COOKER BANANAS FOSTER

The flavors of caramel, rum and walnut naturally complement fresh bananas in this easy version of a dessert classic. It's my go-to choice for any family get-together.
—*Crystal Jo Bruns*

PREP: 10 MIN. • **COOK:** 2 HOURS
MAKES: 5 SERVINGS

- 5 medium firm bananas
- 1 cup packed brown sugar
- ¼ cup butter, melted
- ¼ cup rum
- 1 tsp. vanilla extract
- ½ tsp. ground cinnamon
- ⅓ cup chopped walnuts
- ⅓ cup sweetened shredded coconut
- Optional: Vanilla ice cream or sliced pound cake

1. Cut bananas in half lengthwise, then widthwise; layer in the bottom of a 1½-qt. slow cooker. Combine brown sugar, butter, rum, vanilla and cinnamon; pour over bananas. Cover and cook on low until heated through, about 1½ hours.

2. Sprinkle with walnuts and coconut; cook 30 minutes longer. Serve with ice cream or pound cake if desired.

1 SERVING 462 cal., 17g fat (8g sat. fat), 24mg chol., 99mg sod., 74g carb. (59g sugars, 4g fiber), 3g pro.

KEY LIME CREAM PIE

I am very proud of this luscious no-bake beauty. It's so cool and refreshing—perfect for any summer potluck or get-together. Wherever I take this pie, it quickly disappears, and everyone asks for the recipe.
—Shirley Rickis

PREP: 40 MIN. + CHILLING
MAKES: 12 SERVINGS

- 1 pkg. (11.3 oz.) pecan shortbread cookies, crushed (about 2 cups)
- ⅓ cup butter, melted
- 4 cups heavy whipping cream
- ¼ cup confectioners' sugar
- 1 tsp. coconut extract
- 1 pkg. (8 oz.) cream cheese, softened
- 1 can (14 oz.) sweetened condensed milk
- ½ cup Key lime juice
- ¼ cup sweetened shredded coconut, toasted
- Sliced Key limes, optional

1. In a small bowl, mix crushed cookies and butter. Press onto bottom and up side of a greased 9-in. deep-dish pie plate. In a large bowl, beat cream until it begins to thicken. Add confectioners' sugar and extract; beat until stiff peaks form. In another large bowl, beat cream cheese, condensed milk and lime juice until blended. Fold in 2 cups whipped cream. Spoon into prepared crust.

2. Top with remaining whipped cream; sprinkle with toasted coconut. Refrigerate for at least 4 hours before serving. If desired, garnish with sliced Key limes.

1 PIECE 646 cal., 52g fat (30g sat. fat), 143mg chol., 252mg sod., 41g carb. (29g sugars, 0 fiber), 8g pro.

INGREDIENT SPOTLIGHT

Smaller and more aromatic than regular Persian limes, Key limes have thin skins, lots of seeds, and a bright, tart snap that makes desserts sing. Use freshly squeezed juice (and a little zest) for the best perfume; the classic pie filling's pale yellow color comes naturally—no food coloring needed.

OHIO
CINCINNATI
CHILI, P. 76

THE HEARTLAND

In the Midwest and Great Plains, rich farmland and diverse seasons lead to simple, hearty cooking based on local meats and veggies. Rib-sticking suppers, cozy tavern bites and sweets made from pantry staples all add up to pure comfort.

BRANDY OLD-FASHIONED SWEET

Here in Wisconsin, we make this old-fashioned fave with brandy instead of whiskey and soda rather than water. The result: a milder, sweeter cocktail.
—*Jan Briggs*

TAKES: 10 MIN. • **MAKES:** 1 SERVING

- 1 orange slice
- 1 maraschino cherry
- 1½ oz. maraschino cherry juice
- 1 tsp. bitters
- ¼ to ⅓ cup ice cubes
- 1½ oz. brandy
- 2 tsp. water
- 1 tsp. orange juice
- 3 oz. lemon-lime soda

In a rocks glass, muddle orange slice, cherry, cherry juice and bitters. Add ice. Pour in brandy, water, orange juice and soda.
1 SERVING 277 cal., 0 fat (0 sat. fat), 0 chol., 18mg sod., 36g carb. (17g sugars, 0 fiber), 0 pro.

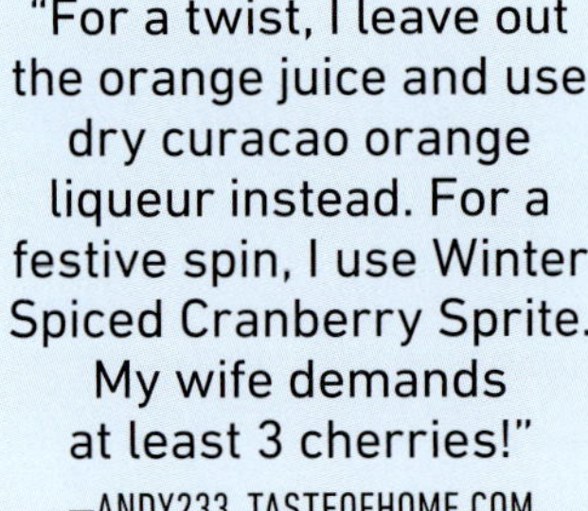

READER REVIEW

★★★★★

"For a twist, I leave out the orange juice and use dry curacao orange liqueur instead. For a festive spin, I use Winter Spiced Cranberry Sprite. My wife demands at least 3 cherries!"
—ANDY233, TASTEOFHOME.COM

EASY BEER & CHEESE DIP

You can use any kind of beer for this recipe. For a lighter beer flavor, go with lager. If you want the beer flavor to be more pronounced, try an ale or wheat beer.
—Taste of Home *Test Kitchen*

TAKES: 15 MIN. • **MAKES:** 3 CUPS

- ¼ cup butter
- ¼ cup all-purpose flour
- ½ tsp. onion powder
- ½ tsp. garlic powder
- ¼ tsp. salt
- Dash white pepper
- 1 cup 2% milk
- ¾ cup beer
- 2 tsp. Dijon mustard
- 1 tsp. Worcestershire sauce
- 2 cups shredded sharp cheddar cheese
- 1 cup shredded Gruyere or Swiss cheese
- Minced chives, optional

1. In a large saucepan, melt butter over medium heat. Whisk in flour, onion powder, garlic powder, salt and pepper until smooth. Gradually whisk in milk and beer. Stir in the mustard and Worcestershire sauce. Bring to a boil; cook and stir until thickened, 1-2 minutes.
2. Reduce heat to low. Add cheese; stir until melted. If desired, garnish with minced chives.
¼ CUP 177 cal., 14g fat (8g sat. fat), 41mg chol., 305mg sod., 4g carb. (2g sugars, 0 fiber), 8g pro.

FRIED CHEESE RAVIOLI

Be sure to make enough of these crispy, coated ravioli. They're bound to be a hit at your party. The golden brown pillows are fun to pick up and dip in marinara sauce.
—Kate Dampier

PREP: 15 MIN. • **COOK:** 20 MIN.
MAKES: ABOUT 2½ DOZEN

- 1 pkg. (9 oz.) refrigerated cheese ravioli
- 1 large egg
- 1 cup seasoned bread crumbs
- ¼ cup shredded Parmesan cheese
- 1½ tsp. dried basil
- ½ cup canola oil
- Additional shredded Parmesan cheese, optional
- 1 cup marinara sauce or meatless spaghetti sauce, warmed

1. Cook ravioli according to package directions; drain and pat dry. In a shallow bowl, lightly beat egg. In another shallow bowl, combine bread crumbs, Parmesan cheese and basil. Dip ravioli in egg, then in bread crumb mixture.
2. In a large skillet or deep-fat fryer, heat ¼ cup oil over medium heat. Fry ravioli in batches until golden brown and crispy, 30-60 seconds on each side; drain on paper towels. Halfway through frying, replace oil; wipe skillet with paper towels if necessary.
3. Sprinkle ravioli with additional cheese if desired. Serve with marinara sauce.

1 RAVIOLI WITH 1½ TSP. SAUCE
58 cal., 2g fat (1g sat. fat), 11mg chol., 158mg sod., 7g carb. (1g sugars, 1g fiber), 2g pro.

TURKEY WILD RICE SOUP

Two Minnesota delicacies, turkey and wild rice, are the stars of this sensational soup. Be prepared to serve seconds!
—Terri Holmgren

PREP: 10 MIN. • **COOK:** 35 MIN.
MAKES: 12 SERVINGS (3 QT.)

- ½ cup butter, cubed
- 2 carrots, finely chopped
- 2 celery ribs, finely chopped
- 1 medium onion, chopped
- ½ cup all-purpose flour
- 4 cups chicken or turkey broth
- 2 cups cooked wild rice
- 2 cups cubed cooked turkey
- 2 cups half-and-half cream
- 1 tsp. dried parsley flakes
- ½ tsp. salt
- ¼ tsp. pepper

1. In a Dutch oven, heat butter over medium-high heat. Add carrots, celery and onion; cook and stir until tender.
2. Stir in flour until blended; cook until bubbly. Gradually stir in broth. Bring to a boil, stirring constantly; cook and stir 1-2 minutes or until thickened.
3. Stir in remaining ingredients; return to a boil. Reduce heat; simmer, uncovered, 20 minutes, stirring occasionally.
1 CUP 222 cal., 13g fat (8g sat. fat), 58mg chol., 533mg sod., 14g carb. (3g sugars, 1g fiber), 11g pro.

INGREDIENT SPOTLIGHT

Wild rice isn't rice at all—it's an ancient aquatic grass native to the Great Lakes region of the northern U.S. and southern Canada. It has long been a vital food for native Ojibwe and Sioux/Dakota communities, and its annual harvest remains culturally and economically important in the region. Wild rice's nutty chew shines in soups, pilafs, meatballs and more.

BEER-BATTERED FISH

Make your own fish fry at home using a classic beer batter. If you're not a drinker, use nonalcoholic beer. Serve with fries, coleslaw and rye bread for a traditional restaurant combo.
—Taste of Home *Test Kitchen*

PREP: 10 MIN. • **COOK:** 5 MIN./BATCH
MAKES: 4 SERVINGS

Oil for deep-fat frying
1 cup all-purpose flour
1½ tsp. baking powder
¾ tsp. salt
½ tsp. garlic powder
¼ tsp. paprika
¼ tsp. pepper
1 cup very cold beer or nonalcoholic beer
1 large egg, lightly beaten
4 cod fillets (6 oz. each)
Optional: Tartar sauce and lemon wedges

1. In an electric skillet or deep fryer, heat oil to 375°. In a shallow bowl, combine flour, baking powder and seasonings. Stir in beer and egg until smooth. Dip fillets in batter; allow excess to drip off.
2. Fry fish in hot oil in batches until golden brown, 2-3 minutes on each side. Drain on paper towels. If desired, serve with tartar sauce and lemon wedges.
1 FILLET 338 cal., 20g fat (2g sat. fat), 79mg chol., 285mg sod., 8g carb. (1g sugars, 0 fiber), 28g pro.

BRATS WITH SAUERKRAUT

I've made many variations of this excellent main dish. It would be popular at a party or potluck. The bratwurst can be plain, smoked or cheese-flavored, and served whole or cut in slices with a bun or without.
—Darlene Dixon

PREP: 10 MIN. • **COOK:** 6 HOURS
MAKES: 8 SERVINGS

8 uncooked bratwurst links
1 can (14 oz.) sauerkraut, rinsed and well drained
2 medium apples, peeled and finely chopped
3 bacon strips, cooked and crumbled
¼ cup packed brown sugar
¼ cup finely chopped onion
1 tsp. ground mustard
8 brat buns, split

1. Place the sausage in a 5-qt. slow cooker. In a large bowl, combine the sauerkraut, apples, bacon, brown sugar, onion and mustard; spoon over bratwurst.
2. Cook, covered, on low until a thermometer inserted in the sausage reads 160°, 6-8 hours.
3. Place brats in buns. Using a slotted spoon, top with sauerkraut mixture.
1 SERVING 534 cal., 28g fat (11g sat. fat), 53mg chol., 1188mg sod., 51g carb. (18g sugars, 4g fiber), 21g pro.

CHICAGO DEEP-DISH PIZZA

My husband and I tried to duplicate the pizza from a popular Chicago restaurant, and I think our recipe turned out even better. The secret is baking your pizza in a cast-iron skillet.
—Lynn Hamilton

PREP: 35 MIN. + RISING
BAKE: 40 MIN.
MAKES: 2 PIZZAS (8 SERVINGS EACH)

- 3½ cups all-purpose flour
- ¼ cup cornmeal
- 1 pkg. (¼ oz.) quick-rise yeast
- 1½ tsp. sugar
- ½ tsp. salt
- 1 cup water
- ⅓ cup olive oil

TOPPINGS

- 6 cups shredded part-skim mozzarella cheese, divided
- 1 can (28 oz.) diced tomatoes, well drained
- 1 can (8 oz.) tomato sauce
- 1 can (6 oz.) tomato paste
- ½ tsp. salt
- ¼ tsp. each garlic powder, dried oregano, dried basil and pepper
- 1 lb. bulk Italian sausage
- 48 slices pepperoni
- ½ lb. sliced fresh mushrooms
- ¼ cup grated Parmesan cheese

1. In a large bowl, combine 1½ cups flour, cornmeal, yeast, sugar and salt. In a saucepan, heat water and oil to 120°-130°. Add to dry ingredients; beat just until moistened. Add the remaining 2 cups flour to form a stiff dough.

2. Turn onto a floured surface; knead until smooth and elastic, 6-8 minutes. Place in a greased bowl, turning once to grease top. Cover and let rise in warm place until doubled, about 30 minutes.

3. Punch down dough; divide in half. Roll each portion into an 11-in. circle. Press dough into the bottoms and up the sides of 2 greased 10-in. cast-iron or other ovenproof skillets. Sprinkle each with 2 cups mozzarella cheese.

4. In a large bowl, combine the tomatoes, tomato sauce, tomato paste and seasonings. Spoon 1½ cups over each pizza. Layer each pizza with half each of the sausage, pepperoni and mushrooms, and 1 cup of the mozzarella. Sprinkle each with 2 Tbsp. Parmesan cheese.

5. Cover and bake at 450° for 35 minutes. Uncover; bake until lightly browned, about 5 minutes longer.

NOTE Two 9-in. springform pans may be used in place of the skillets. Place pans on baking sheets to bake. Run a knife around edge of pan to loosen crust before removing side of pan.

1 PIECE 407 cal., 23g fat (9g sat. fat), 49mg chol., 872mg sod., 32g carb. (4g sugars, 2g fiber), 20g pro.

WINDY CITY SLICE

Born of Chicago cravings and perfected in a cast-iron skillet, this pie recipe layers a tall, tender crust with plenty of hearty toppings. Many pizzerias finish their pies with crushed tomatoes on top. If you want that classic, caramelized tomato look, put the tomatoes on last before baking the pie. Let the pizza rest 10–15 minutes before cutting so the slices stand tall.

OKTOBERFEST CASSEROLE

In northeastern Ohio, we love German flavors. This delicious casserole is a trifecta mashup of my favorite dishes. It combines the flavors of a cheesy hash brown casserole with bratwursts and sauerkraut, plus pretzels and beer cheese. It takes just 15 minutes to mix and uses only one bowl. It's sure to please everyone any time of the year.
—*Sarah Markley*

PREP: 15 MIN.
BAKE: 1½ HOURS + STANDING
MAKES: 12 SERVINGS

- 2 cans (10½ oz. each) condensed cheddar cheese soup, undiluted
- 1 cup beer or chicken broth
- 1 cup sour cream
- 1 pkg. (32 oz.) frozen cubed hash brown potatoes, thawed
- 1 can (14 oz.) sauerkraut, rinsed and well drained
- 2 cups shredded cheddar cheese
- 1 pkg. (14 oz.) fully cooked bratwurst links, chopped
- 2 cups pretzel pieces

1. Preheat oven to 350°. In a large bowl, whisk soup, beer and sour cream until combined. Stir in potatoes, sauerkraut, cheese and chopped bratwurst. Transfer to a greased 13x9-in. baking dish. Cover and bake for 45 minutes.
2. Uncover; bake 30 minutes. Top with pretzel pieces. Bake casserole until bubbly and heated through, 12-15 minutes longer. Let stand 10 minutes before serving.
FREEZE OPTION Freeze cooled potato mixture in freezer containers. To use, partially thaw in refrigerator overnight. Heat through in a saucepan, stirring occasionally; add broth or water if necessary.
1 SERVING 356 cal., 21g fat (10g sat. fat), 49mg chol., 884mg sod., 29g carb. (4g sugars, 3g fiber), 13g pro.

CHILI CONEY DOGS

From the youngest kids to the oldest adults, everyone in our family loves these hot dogs. They're so easy to throw together in the morning or even the night before.
—Michele Harris

PREP: 20 MIN. • **COOK:** 4 HOURS
MAKES: 8 SERVINGS

- 1 lb. lean ground beef (90% lean)
- 1 can (15 oz.) tomato sauce
- ½ cup water
- 2 Tbsp. Worcestershire sauce
- 1 Tbsp. dried minced onion
- ½ tsp. garlic powder
- ½ tsp. ground mustard
- ½ tsp. chili powder
- ½ tsp. pepper
- Dash cayenne pepper
- 8 hot dogs
- 8 hot dog buns, split
- Optional toppings: Shredded cheddar cheese, relish, mustard and chopped onion

1. In a large skillet, cook beef over medium heat until no longer pink, 6-8 minutes, breaking into crumbles; drain. Stir in tomato sauce, water, Worcestershire sauce, dried minced onion and seasonings.

2. Place hot dogs in a 3-qt. slow cooker; top with beef mixture. Cook, covered, on low 4-5 hours or until heated through. Serve on buns with toppings as desired.

1 CHILI DOG 371 cal., 20g fat (8g sat. fat), 53mg chol., 992mg sod., 26g carb. (5g sugars, 2g fiber), 21g pro.

CINCINNATI CHILI

My husband had this type of chili when visiting a friend in Ohio and was thrilled when a friend gave me a recipe. I made a few tweaks, and it was a big hit. Make the sauce ahead and freeze it, and you can have dinner on the table in the time it takes to boil spaghetti. A quick tossed salad completes the meal.
—Tari Ambler

PREP: 15 MIN. • **COOK:** 2 HOURS
MAKES: 5 SERVINGS

- 2 lbs. ground beef
- 2 medium onions, chopped
- 2 cups water
- 1 can (8 oz.) tomato sauce
- 1 can (6 oz.) tomato paste
- 3 Tbsp. chili powder
- ½ oz. unsweetened chocolate, chopped
- 4 garlic cloves, minced
- 2 Tbsp. cider vinegar
- 2 tsp. Worcestershire sauce
- 1 bay leaf
- 1 tsp. salt
- 1 tsp. ground cumin
- 1 tsp. ground cinnamon
- ½ tsp. ground allspice
- ¼ tsp. ground cloves
- ⅛ to ¼ tsp. cayenne pepper
- Optional: Hot cooked spaghetti, shredded cheddar cheese, additional chopped onion, rinsed and drained kidney beans and oyster crackers

1. In a Dutch oven over medium heat, cook beef and onions until beef is no longer pink and onions are tender, 10-12 minutes, breaking meat into crumbles; drain. Add the next 15 ingredients. Bring to a boil; reduce heat.

2. Simmer, uncovered, 1¾ hours or until the desired consistency is achieved, stirring occasionally. Discard bay leaf. If desired, serve with spaghetti, cheese, additional chopped onion, kidney beans and oyster crackers.

1 CUP 431 cal., 24g fat (9g sat. fat), 112mg chol., 967mg sod., 18g carb. (6g sugars, 5g fiber), 37g pro.

ST. LOUIS-STYLE PIZZA

Provel cheese and a cracker-thin crust are the hallmarks of St. Louis-style pizza. Provel cheese is a processed blend of cheddar, Swiss and provolone that originated in St. Louis. It melts at a low temperature, which means it stays ooey-gooey after the pizza is out of the oven and on the dinner table. Don't forget to cut your pizza as they would in Missouri—square pieces only!
—Taste of Home *Test Kitchen*

PREP: 15 MIN. + STANDING
BAKE: 30 MIN.
MAKES: 2 PIZZAS (4 SERVINGS EACH)

- 2 cups all-purpose flour
- 2 tsp. baking powder
- ½ tsp. salt
- 8 to 10 Tbsp. water
- 2 Tbsp. olive oil
- ⅔ cup crushed tomatoes in puree
- 2 Tbsp. tomato paste
- ½ tsp. sugar
- ½ tsp. dried basil
- ¼ tsp. dried oregano
- 12 oz. Provel cheese, shredded or 1½ cups shredded white cheddar plus 1 cup shredded provolone plus 1 cup shredded Swiss
- 1 pkg. (3½ oz.) sliced pepperoni
- 1 small green pepper, thinly sliced
- ½ small red onion, thinly sliced

1. In a large bowl, whisk flour, baking powder and salt. Stir in water and oil until combined. Turn onto a lightly floured surface. Gently form into a ball. Cover and let rest 10 minutes. Divide dough in half. On parchment, roll each half into a 10-in. circle. Leaving dough on parchment, transfer each circle to a 12-in. pizza pan.

2. Preheat oven to 425°. Combine crushed tomatoes, tomato paste, sugar, basil and oregano; spread over crusts. Top with cheese, pepperoni, green pepper and onion. If desired, sprinkle with additional dried basil and oregano. Bake on a low oven rack, 1 pizza at a time, until bottom of crust is golden and cheese is lightly browned, 15-20 minutes. Cut into squares.

1 SERVING 382 cal., 23g fat (10g sat. fat), 50mg chol., 755mg sod., 28g carb. (2g sugars, 2g fiber), 17g pro.

ORIGIN STORY

In the years following World War II, St. Louis's Italian neighborhoods started topping ultrathin, crackerlike crusts with locally created Provel cheese. When former tile setter Ed Imo opened his pizzeria in 1964, he cut Imo's Pizza pies into small "party cut" tiles—perfect for sharing. The signature shape makes St. Louis pizza easy to eat with one hand—while holding a drink in the other.

NEBRASKA RUNZAS

Runzas are a classic comfort food in Nebraska. They're made simply at home with frozen dinner rolls and just a few other ingredients, resulting in tasty and satisfying hand-held pockets of goodness.
—Sharon Arp

PREP: 30 MIN. + RISING
BAKE: 20 MIN.
MAKES: 16 SERVINGS

- 1 pkg. (48 oz.) frozen Texas-size white dinner rolls
- 2 Tbsp. butter
- 1½ lbs. ground beef
- 1 cup chopped onion
- 3 Tbsp. beef bouillon granules
- 1 bag (14 oz.) coleslaw mix

1. Place rolls on parchment-lined baking sheets; cover with plastic wrap coated with cooking spray; let rise until doubled.
2. Preheat oven to 350°. In a large skillet, heat butter over medium heat. Cook beef and onion over medium heat, crumbling beef, until meat is no longer pink. Add beef bouillon granules and cabbage mix. Cook until cabbage is tender, 5 minutes longer. Strain; cool completely.
3. On a lightly floured surface, roll each dinner roll into a 5-in. oval. Place about ¼ cup of meat mixture in the center. Fold dough over filling, pressing edges to seal. Place seam side down on greased baking sheets. Repeat with the remaining rolls and meat mixture.
4. Prick tops with a fork. Bake until golden brown, 20-23 minutes.

1 ROLL 327 cal., 10g fat (3g sat. fat), 30mg chol., 753mg sod., 45g carb. (6g sugars, 2g fiber), 14g pro.

MAKE IT A MORNING RUNZA

For a grab-and-go breakfast runza, brown breakfast sausage instead of ground beef with the onion. Fold in soft scrambled eggs and a little shredded cheese, then tuck into the dough and bake as directed.

HOT POCKET OF THE PLAINS

Soft rolls filled with beef, onion and cabbage came to the Plains with Volga German immigrants in the 1870s. They got their name in 1949 at the first Runza restaurant in Lincoln. Today, they're a Cornhusker game-day classic.

WISCONSIN BUTTER BURGERS

Butter burgers are a beloved Wisconsin comfort food most often found at Culver's, a popular Midwestern fast food chain. They're often served with piping hot fried cheese curds, another Wisconsin favorite.
—*Margaret Knoebel*

TAKES: 30 MIN.
MAKES: 4 SERVINGS

- 1 lb. lean ground beef (90% lean)
- ½ tsp. salt
- ½ tsp. pepper
- 5 Tbsp. butter, divided
- 4 hamburger buns, split
- 4 slices cheddar cheese, optional
- Optional toppings: Tomato slices, lettuce leaves, sliced onion, dill pickle slices, ketchup and mustard

1. Shape beef into 4 patties, each ½-in. thick. Sprinkle patties with salt and pepper.

2. Working in batches if needed, heat butter in a large skillet or griddle over medium heat. With a heavy metal spatula or burger press, flatten each patty to ¼-in. thickness. Cook until edges start to brown, about 1½ minutes; flip burgers. Cook until well browned and a thermometer reads at least 160°, about 1 minute longer. If desired, top with a slice of cheddar cheese. Remove from pan; keep warm. Add 2 Tbsp. butter to the same pan, repeat with remaining beef patties.

3. Add remaining 1 Tbsp. of butter to the pan; add bun, cut side down. Toast until golden brown.

4. Transfer burgers to toasted buns and serve with desired toppings.

1 BURGER 429 cal., 26g fat (13g sat. fat), 109mg chol., 686mg sod., 22g carb. (3g sugars, 1g fiber), 26g pro.

WINNING APPLE CRISP

Central Wisconsin is apple country, and making delicious apple crisp is one way to use the fruit. This simple treat doesn't take much time to assemble.
—Gertrude Bartnick

PREP: 20 MIN. • **BAKE:** 1 HOUR
MAKES: 8 SERVINGS

- 1 cup all-purpose flour
- ¾ cup rolled oats
- 1 cup packed brown sugar
- 1 tsp. ground cinnamon
- ½ cup butter, softened
- 4 cups chopped peeled apples
- 1 cup sugar
- 2 Tbsp. cornstarch
- 1 cup water
- 1 tsp. vanilla extract
- Vanilla ice cream, optional

1. Preheat oven to 350°. In a large bowl, combine first 4 ingredients. Cut in butter until crumbly. Press half the crumb mixture into a greased 2½-qt. baking dish or a 9-in. square baking pan. Cover with apples.
2. In a small saucepan, combine the sugar, cornstarch, water and vanilla. Bring to a boil; cook and stir 2 minutes or until thick and clear. Pour over apples. Sprinkle with the remaining crumb mixture.
3. Bake until apples are tender, 60-65 minutes. Serve warm, with ice cream if desired.

1 SERVING 426 cal., 12g fat (7g sat. fat), 31mg chol., 127mg sod., 79g carb. (58g sugars, 2g fiber), 3g pro.

WINNING PEAR CRISP Substitute pears for the apples.

SOUTH DAKOTA FRITO TREATS

Yep, they're made with corn chips! These salty sweets were a staple after meetings of the quilt guild I belonged to in South Dakota.
—Carol Tramp

PREP: 15 MIN. + STANDING
MAKES: 2 DOZEN

- 2 pkg. (9¾ oz. each) corn chips, divided
- 2 cups semisweet chocolate chips, divided
- 1 cup sugar
- 1 cup light corn syrup
- 1 cup creamy peanut butter

1. Spread 1 package corn chips on the bottom of a greased 13x9-in. baking pan; sprinkle 1 cup chocolate chips over the top.
2. In a large heavy saucepan, combine sugar and corn syrup. Bring to a boil; cook and stir 1 minute. Remove from heat; stir in peanut butter. Pour half the peanut butter mixture over the chip mixture. Top with remaining package corn chips and 1 cup chocolate chips; drizzle with the remaining peanut butter mixture. Let stand until set. Cut into bars.

1 BAR 337 cal., 18g fat (5g sat. fat), 0 chol., 196mg sod., 43g carb. (29g sugars, 2g fiber), 5g pro.

CRANBERRY CHEESECAKE

Every year when the cranberries are harvested, my family looks forward to eating this cheesecake.
—Nairda Monroe

PREP: 30 MIN.
BAKE: 55 MIN. + CHILLING
MAKES: 12 SERVINGS

- 2 cups graham cracker or shortbread cookie crumbs
- ⅓ cup butter, melted

TOPPING

- 2 cups fresh or frozen cranberries
- ⅔ cup sugar
- ⅓ cup water
- 1 tsp. lemon juice

FILLING

- 4 pkg. (8 oz. each) cream cheese, softened
- 1 cup sugar
- 1 Tbsp. lemon juice
- 5 large eggs, room temperature, lightly beaten

Optional garnish: Sugared Cranberries

1. Preheat oven to 325°. Place a greased 9-in. springform pan on a double thickness of heavy-duty foil (about 18 in. square). Wrap foil securely around pan. Place on a baking sheet.

2. In a small bowl, mix cracker crumbs and butter; press into bottom of prepared pan. Bake 6 minutes. Cool on a wire rack.

3. Meanwhile, in a large saucepan, combine cranberries, sugar and water. Cook, uncovered, over medium heat until berries pop, 12-15 minutes. Add lemon juice. Press cranberry mixture through a mesh strainer into a small bowl; discard pulp and seeds. Set strained mixture aside.

4. For filling, in a large bowl, beat cream cheese, sugar and lemon juice until smooth. Add eggs; beat on low speed just until blended. Pour into crust. Spoon ¼ cup topping over filling; cut through filling with a knife to swirl. Place springform pan in a larger pan; add 1 in. of hot water to larger pan.

5. Bake 55-65 minutes or until center is just set and top appears dull. Remove springform pan from water bath; remove foil. Cool cheesecake on a wire rack for 10 minutes. Carefully run a knife around edge of pan to loosen; cool 1 hour longer. Pour remaining cranberry topping over cheesecake. Refrigerate cheesecake overnight, covering when completely cooled. Remove rim from pan. Garnish with sugared cranberries if desired.

1 PIECE 522 cal., 35g fat (19g sat. fat), 174mg chol., 423mg sod., 46g carb. (35g sugars, 1g fiber), 8g pro.

SUGARED CRANBERRIES In a large saucepan, bring ¼ cup water and 6 Tbsp. sugar to a simmer over medium heat; stir until sugar is dissolved and mixture begins to thicken, 5-7 minutes. Stir in 1¾ cups fresh or thawed cranberries; remove from heat and stir until cranberries are coated. Use a slotted spoon to transfer cranberries to a parchment-lined baking sheet. Let stand for 1 hour. Place remaining 6 Tbsp. sugar in a large bowl. Add cranberries; toss to coat.

READER REVIEW

★★★★★

"Always turns out perfect. I've served this one to many different people and have received rave reviews. Friends and family frequently ask for it. Well worth the effort spent preparing the cranberries."

—TELX2, TASTEOFHOME.COM

TEXAS
CLASSIC TEXAS
CAVIAR, P. 85

TEXAS & SOUTHWEST

Where cowboy country meets desert plateaus, the cooking is shaped by cattle drives, intense heat and deep cultural ties to Mexico. From sizzling fajitas and roasted chiles to cool drinks and caramelly sweets, the Southwest's flavors are comforting and bold.

BISCOCHITO MARTINI

This sweet delight will melt in your mouth just as if you were taking a big bite of a fresh homemade biscochito cookie. Make sure you shake the martini well.
—Letitia Montoya

TAKES: 5 MIN. • **MAKES:** 1 SERVING

- Optional: Honey and biscochito or snickerdoodle cookie crumbs
- Ice cubes
- 1½ oz. vanilla vodka
- 1½ oz. RumChata liqueur
- 1 oz. anise liqueur

1. If desired, place honey on a plate; place cookie crumbs on second plate. Hold chilled glass upside down and dip rim in honey, then in crushed cookie crumbs.
2. Fill a shaker three-fourths full with ice. Add vodka and liqueurs; cover and shake until condensation forms on outside of shaker, 10-15 seconds. Strain into prepared glass.
1 SERVING 347 cal., 17g fat (10g sat. fat), 61mg chol., 17mg sod., 6g carb. (0 sugars, 0 fiber), 1g pro.

CLASSIC TEXAS CAVIAR

I adapted this Texas Caviar from one in a cookbook I received a long time ago, and now I can't imagine a get-together at my house without this quick and healthy appetizer.
—Becky Oliver

PREP: 20 MIN. + CHILLING
MAKES: 20 SERVINGS (5 CUPS)

- 2 cans (15½ oz. each) black-eyed peas, rinsed and drained
- 1 can (10 oz.) diced tomatoes and green chiles, drained
- 1 medium green pepper, finely chopped
- 1 cup fresh whole kernel corn or frozen shoepeg corn, thawed
- 1 small red onion, finely chopped
- ½ cup Italian salad dressing
- 2 Tbsp. lime juice
- ¼ tsp. salt
- ¼ tsp. pepper
- 1 medium ripe avocado, peeled and cubed
- Tortilla chips

1. In a large bowl, combine the peas, tomatoes, green pepper, corn and onion. In a small bowl, whisk the dressing, lime juice, salt and pepper. Pour over the black-eyed pea mixture and stir to coat. Cover and refrigerate for at least 1 hour.
2. Stir in avocado just before serving. Serve with chips.
¼ CUP 68 cal., 2g fat (0 sat. fat), 0 chol., 200mg sod., 10g carb. (2g sugars, 2g fiber), 3g pro.

RANCH WATER

Three simple ingredients come together to make ranch water, your new go-to summer cocktail. Essential to the drink, the Topo Chico brings refreshing mineral flavor and tons of bubbles.
—Caroline Stanko

TAKES: 5 MIN. • **MAKES:** 1 SERVING

- Ice cubes
- 2 oz. blanco tequila
- ½ lime
- 1 can Topo Chico mineral water
- 1 lime slice, optional

Fill highball glass about two-thirds full with ice. Add tequila; squeeze lime into glass. Top with mineral water and stir. If desired, garnish with lime slice.
1 SERVING 130 cal., 0 fat (0 sat. fat), 0 chol., 1mg sod., 0 carb. (0 sugars, 0 fiber), 0 pro.

ORIGIN STORY

Legend has it Ranch Water was first mixed by ranch hands in West Texas in the 1960s to slake a hard day's thirst. Since then, it's become a Texas staple—showing up everywhere from dive bars and cocktail lounges to poolside menus across the state.

CHICKEN FAJITAS

This recipe is in my weeknight dinner rotation. The marinated chicken in these popular wraps is truly mouthwatering. The fajitas go together in a snap and always get raves!
—Julie Sterchi

PREP: 20 MIN. + MARINATING
COOK: 10 MIN.
MAKES: 6 SERVINGS

- 4 Tbsp. canola oil, divided
- 2 Tbsp. lemon juice
- 1½ tsp. seasoned salt
- 1½ tsp. dried oregano
- 1½ tsp. ground cumin
- 1 tsp. garlic powder
- ½ tsp. chili powder
- ½ tsp. paprika
- ½ tsp. crushed red pepper flakes, optional
- 1½ lbs. boneless skinless chicken breasts, cut into thin strips
- ½ medium sweet red pepper, julienned
- ½ medium green pepper, julienned
- 4 green onions, thinly sliced
- ½ cup chopped onion
- 6 flour tortillas (8 in.), warmed
- Optional: Shredded cheddar cheese, taco sauce, salsa, guacamole, sliced red onions and sour cream

1. In a large bowl, combine 2 Tbsp. oil, lemon juice and seasonings; add chicken. Turn to coat; cover. Refrigerate 1-4 hours.

2. In a large cast-iron or other heavy skillet, saute peppers and onions in remaining 2 Tbsp. oil until crisp-tender. Remove and keep warm.

3. Drain the chicken, discarding marinade. In the same skillet, cook chicken over medium-high heat until no longer pink, 5-6 minutes. Return pepper mixture to pan; heat through.

4. Spoon filling down centers of tortillas; add toppings as desired. Fold in half.

1 FAJITA 369 cal., 15g fat (2g sat. fat), 63mg chol., 689mg sod., 30g carb. (2g sugars, 1g fiber), 28g pro.

CUSTOMIZE YOUR FAJITAS

- **Swap proteins.** Use steak strips, shrimp or a chicken-shrimp mix.
- **Go veg.** Load up peppers and onions; add garbanzo beans, cactus (nopales), squash or tofu.
- **Make a bowl or wraps.** Try Bibb lettuce wraps, or make a salad with greens, black beans, corn and guacamole.

RIBEYES WITH HATCH CHILE BUTTER

In summer, succulent ribeye steaks call for my flavor-packed compound butter, swirled with Hatch chiles, cilantro, lime juice and garlic.
—David Ross

PREP: 45 MIN. • **GRILL:** 10 MIN.
MAKES: 6 SERVINGS

- 2 whole green chiles, such as Hatch or poblano peppers
- 1 cup minced fresh cilantro
- ½ cup butter, softened
- 2 garlic cloves, minced
- 2 tsp. minced fresh oregano
- 1 Tbsp. lime juice
- ½ tsp. salt, divided
- ½ tsp. pepper, divided
- 3 lbs. beef ribeye steaks
- 1 Tbsp. olive oil
- 1 tsp. coarse sea salt
- Pickled jalapeno slices, optional

1. Cut peppers lengthwise in half. Remove stems and seeds; flatten slightly. Grill chiles, skin side down, until skins blister, about 3 minutes. Immediately place peppers in a small bowl; let stand, covered, 20 minutes.
2. Peel off and discard charred skin. Place grilled peppers, cilantro, butter, garlic, oregano, lime juice, ¼ tsp. salt and ¼ tsp. pepper in a food processor; pulse until just combined. Refrigerate until firm.
3. Brush the steaks with oil and sprinkle with remaining ¼ tsp. salt and ¼ tsp. pepper. Grill, covered, over medium-high heat or broil 4 in. from heat until meat reaches desired doneness (for medium-rare, a thermometer should read 135°; medium, 140°; medium-well, 145°), about 4 minutes on each side. Let stand 5 minutes. Cut into thin slices.
4. Meanwhile, in a small saucepan, melt half the chile butter. Drizzle over steaks. Serve remaining butter with steaks. Sprinkle with coarse sea salt. If desired, garnish with jalapeno slices and additional oregano.

NOTE Wear disposable gloves when cutting hot peppers; the oils can burn skin. Avoid touching your face.

5 OZ. COOKED BEEF WITH 5 TSP. BUTTER 657 cal., 53g fat (25g sat. fat), 174mg chol., 815mg sod., 2g carb. (0 sugars, 0 fiber), 40g pro.

INGREDIENT SPOTLIGHT

Grown in New Mexico's Hatch Valley, the famous Hatch chile peppers have a distinctly deep and smoky taste when roasted. Peak season hits late August to early September, when many markets offer raw and fire-roasted peppers. They're fantastic folded into eggs, stirred into beans or blended into butters and salsas.

EASY FRY BREAD TACOS

My niece gave me this hearty recipe. Frozen bread dough makes the tacos easy to prep.
—Robin Wells

PREP: 10 MIN. + RISING
COOK: 45 MIN.
MAKES: 12 SERVINGS

- 1 loaf frozen white bread dough, thawed

TOPPING

- 1 lb. ground beef
- 1 lb. hot bulk pork sausage
- 1 envelope taco seasoning
- 1 can (15 oz.) pinto beans, rinsed and drained
- ½ cup water
- Oil for deep-fat frying
- Optional toppings: Chopped tomato, finely chopped onion, shredded lettuce, shredded cheddar cheese and taco sauce

1. Allow dough to rise according to package directions. Meanwhile, for topping, cook beef and sausage in a skillet over medium heat until no longer pink, breaking the meat into crumbles; drain. Stir in the taco seasoning, beans and water. Simmer 15-20 minutes or until water is almost evaporated; set aside.

2. After dough rises, punch down. Divide dough into 12 equal balls. Using a small amount of flour, roll each ball into a 6-in. circle (dough will be thin).

3. In an electric skillet or deep fryer, heat 1 in. oil to 350°. Gently place 1 dough circle into oil. Fry until golden brown, 1-2 minutes, turning once. Drain bread on paper towels; keep warm. Serve with toppings as desired.

1 TACO 373 cal., 22g fat (5g sat. fat), 44mg chol., 777mg sod., 27g carb. (2g sugars, 3g fiber), 16g pro.

READER REVIEW

★★★★★

"My friend who is Hopi-Navajo made these at one of our group campouts. She also did them as a dessert served with powdered sugar and cinnamon, and with honey. She said the people on the reservation prefer Blue Bird flour to make their fry bread. Blue Bird is available in most supermarkets in Arizona and the surrounding states."

—WOOCHER, TASTEOFHOME.COM

NAVAJO FRY BREAD

Fry bread was born of necessity after the 1864 Long Walk to Bosque Redondo, New Mexico, where Navajo families cooked from government rations on land unfit for growing their traditional crops. The chapter ended in 1868, but fry bread endured. Over time, other Native American nations created their own savory and sweet versions of fry bread.

BEEF-STUFFED SOPAIPILLAS

After my brothers' football games when we were kids, we would all descend on a local restaurant for their wonderful southwestern stuffed soapaipillas. This recipe takes me back to that delicious childhood memory. Even my Canadian husband raves about these!
—Lara Pennell

TAKES: 30 MIN.
MAKES: 4 SERVINGS

- 2 cups all-purpose flour
- 1 tsp. salt
- 1 tsp. baking powder
- ½ cup water
- ¼ cup evaporated milk
- 1½ tsp. canola oil
- Additional oil for frying

FILLING

- 1 lb. ground beef
- ¾ cup chopped onion
- ½ tsp. salt
- ½ tsp. garlic powder
- ¼ tsp. pepper

SAUCE

- 1 can (10¾ oz.) condensed cream of chicken soup, undiluted
- ½ cup chicken broth
- 1 can (4 oz.) chopped green chiles
- ½ tsp. onion powder
- 2 cups shredded cheddar cheese

1. In a large bowl, combine the flour, salt and baking powder. Stir in water, milk and oil with a fork until a ball forms. On a lightly floured surface, knead dough gently for 2-3 minutes. Cover and let stand for 15 minutes. Divide into 4 portions; roll each into a 6½-in. circle.

2. In an electric skillet or deep-fat fryer, heat oil to 375°. Fry circles, 1 at a time, for 2-3 minutes on each side or until golden brown. Drain on paper towels.

3. In a large skillet, cook beef and onion until meat is no longer pink, crumbling beef; drain. Stir in the salt, garlic powder and pepper. In a large saucepan, combine the soup, broth, chiles and onion powder; cook for 10 minutes or until heated through.

4. Cut a slit on 1 side of each sopaipilla; fill with ½ cup of meat mixture. Top with cheese. Serve with sauce.

1 SOPAIPILLA 975 cal., 55g fat (22g sat. fat), 182mg chol., 2265mg sod., 62g carb. (4g sugars, 4g fiber), 54g pro.

SANTA FE SKILLET

As a mother who works full time, I'm always looking for quick, easy meals to prepare. This is a timeless favorite.
—Lorie VanHorn

TAKES: 30 MIN.
MAKES: 6 SERVINGS

- 1 lb. lean ground beef (90% lean)
- 1 small onion, chopped
- 1 pkg. (6 oz.) four-cheese corkscrew pasta mix
- 2 cups salsa
- 1 cup hot water
- 1 Tbsp. chili powder
- ½ tsp. salt
- Dash cayenne pepper
- 1 can (14½ oz.) diced tomatoes, undrained
- 1 can (2¼ oz.) sliced ripe olives, drained
- 1 cup shredded cheddar cheese
- Sour cream, optional

1. In a large skillet, cook beef and onion over medium heat until meat is no longer pink, crumbling beef; drain. Stir in the pasta, contents of seasoning packet, salsa, water, chili powder, salt and cayenne.
2. Bring to a boil. Reduce heat; cover and simmer until pasta is tender, about 15 minutes, adding more water if necessary. Stir in tomatoes; sprinkle with olives and cheese. Cover and simmer until heated through, 3-4 minutes. Serve with sour cream if desired.
NOTE This recipe was tested with Pasta Roni mix.
1¼ CUPS 287 cal., 10g fat (3g sat. fat), 49mg chol., 1061mg sod., 29g carb. (7g sugars, 3g fiber), 19g pro.

SPICY CHUCK WAGON BEANS

Baked beans don't get any easier! All you have to do is open some cans, chop an onion, and add a dash (or two) of hot sauce. They'll simmer to perfection in minutes.
—James Schend

TAKES: 30 MIN.
MAKES: 24 SERVINGS

- 1 Tbsp. canola oil
- 1 medium onion, chopped
- 2 cans (28 oz. each) baked beans
- 3 cans (15 oz. each) chili beans, undrained
- 2 cans (15 oz. each) black beans, rinsed and drained
- 2 pkg. (7 oz. each) frozen fully cooked breakfast sausage links, thawed and cut into ½-in. pieces
- 1 cup beer or reduced-sodium chicken broth
- 2 chipotle peppers in adobo sauce, minced
- 1 to 2 Tbsp. hot pepper sauce

In a Dutch oven, heat oil over medium-high heat; saute onion until tender, 3-5 minutes. Stir in remaining ingredients; bring to a boil. Reduce the heat; simmer, uncovered, until the beans are thickened and flavors are blended, about 15 minutes, stirring occasionally.
⅔ CUP 221 cal., 8g fat (3g sat. fat), 15mg chol., 663mg sod., 30g carb. (2g sugars, 8g fiber), 10g pro.

CLASSIC TRES LECHES CAKE

A classic in Mexican kitchens for generations, this cake gets its name from the three types of milk—evaporated, sweetened condensed and heavy whipping cream—used to create a super moist and tender texture.
—Taste of Home *Test Kitchen*

PREP: 45 MIN.
BAKE: 20 MIN. + CHILLING
MAKES: 10 SERVINGS

- 4 large eggs, separated, room temperature
- ⅔ cup sugar, divided
- ⅔ cup cake flour
- Dash salt
- ¾ cup heavy whipping cream
- ¾ cup evaporated milk
- ¾ cup sweetened condensed milk
- 2 tsp. vanilla extract
- ¼ tsp. rum extract

TOPPING

- 1¼ cups heavy whipping cream
- 3 Tbsp. sugar
- Optional: Dulce de leche or sliced fresh strawberries

1. Place egg whites in a large bowl. Line bottom of a 9-in. springform pan with parchment; grease the paper.
2. Preheat oven to 350°. In another large bowl, beat egg yolks until slightly thickened. Gradually add ⅓ cup sugar, beating on high speed until thick and lemon-colored. Fold in flour, a third at a time.
3. Add salt to egg whites; with clean beaters, beat on medium until soft peaks form. Gradually add the remaining ⅓ cup sugar, 1 Tbsp. at a time, beating on high after each addition until sugar is dissolved. Continue beating until soft glossy peaks form. Fold a third of the whites into batter, then fold in remaining whites. Gently spread into prepared pan.
4. Bake until top springs back when lightly touched, 20-25 minutes. Cool for 10 minutes before removing from pan to a wire rack to cool completely.
5. Place the cake on a rimmed serving plate. Poke holes in top with a skewer. In a small bowl, mix cream, evaporated milk, sweetened condensed milk and extracts; brush or pour slowly over cake. Refrigerate, covered, 2 hours.
6. For topping, beat cream until it begins to thicken. Add sugar; beat until peaks form. Spread over top of cake. If desired, top cake with dulce de leche or strawberries just before serving.

1 PIECE 392 cal., 23g fat (14g sat. fat), 142mg chol., 104mg sod., 40g carb. (33g sugars, 0 fiber), 8g pro.

READER REVIEW

★★★★★

"I've tried other tres leches recipes, and this is a really good one! I used 3 tsp. of vanilla and omitted the rum extract. My family and party guests devoured it!"

—KRISTINECHAYES576, TASTEOFHOME.COM

TEXAS PECAN PIE

I won a blue ribbon for this pie at the Texas State Fair. Since I was in the military for more than 20 years, I didn't really start cooking until after I retired. Now I enjoy spending my time in the kitchen.
—Michelle Shockley

PREP: 25 MIN.
BAKE: 45 MIN. + COOLING
MAKES: 8 SERVINGS

- 1 cup all-purpose flour
- ¼ tsp. salt
- ⅓ cup shortening
- 3 Tbsp. cold water

FILLING

- 1¼ cups chopped pecans
- 1 cup plus 1 Tbsp. light corn syrup
- 3 large eggs
- ½ cup plus 1 Tbsp. sugar
- 1½ tsp. vanilla extract
- Pinch salt

1. In a bowl, combine the flour and salt; cut in shortening until crumbly. Gradually add cold water, tossing with a fork until a ball forms.
2. Roll out dough to fit a 9-in. pie plate. Transfer crust to pie plate. Trim crust to ½ in. beyond edge of plate; flute edge. Sprinkle with pecans.
3. In a small bowl, beat the corn syrup, eggs, sugar, vanilla and salt until well blended. Pour over pecans.
4. Bake at 350° until a knife inserted in the center comes out clean, 45-50 minutes. Cool completely on a wire rack.

1 PIECE 466 cal., 23g fat (4g sat. fat), 80mg chol., 151mg sod., 62g carb. (37g sugars, 2g fiber), 6g pro.

SOPAIPILLAS

Light, crispy pastry puffs, sopaipillas are a sweet way to round out a spicy meal. We love to serve them warm and top them off with honey or sugar.
—Mary Anne McWhirter

PREP: 15 MIN. + STANDING
COOK: 25 MIN. • **MAKES:** 1 DOZEN

- 1 cup all-purpose flour
- 1½ tsp. baking powder
- ¼ tsp. salt
- 1 Tbsp. shortening
- ⅓ cup warm water
- Oil for deep-fat frying
- Optional: Confectioners' sugar and honey

1. In a large bowl, combine flour, baking powder and salt. Cut in shortening until mixture resembles fine crumbs. Gradually add water, tossing with a fork until a loose ball forms (dough will be crumbly).

2. On a lightly floured surface, knead the dough for 3 minutes or until smooth. Cover and let rest for 10 minutes. Roll out into a 12x10-in. rectangle. Cut into 12 square shapes with a knife or cut into 12 circles using a round biscuit cutter.

3. In a deep-fat fryer, heat 2 in. oil to 375°. Fry sopaipillas for 1-2 minutes on each side. Drain on paper towels; keep warm. If desired, dust with confectioners' sugar and/or serve with honey.

1 SOPAIPILLA 57 cal., 2g fat (0 sat. fat), 0 chol., 109mg sod., 8g carb. (0 sugars, 0 fiber), 1g pro.

IDAHO
CAMPFIRE
COBBLER, P. 110

EASY SALMON CAESAR SALAD

The salmon in this simple Caesar salad is lightly seasoned with salt and pepper. This makes the crunchy garlic-salt croutons stand out even more.
—Taste of Home *Test Kitchen*

TAKES: 30 MIN.
MAKES: 4 SERVINGS

- 1 cup cubed French bread
- 1 Tbsp. olive oil
- ¼ tsp. garlic salt
- ⅛ tsp. pepper

SALMON

- 4 salmon fillets (6 oz. each)
- ¾ tsp. salt
- ¼ tsp. pepper
- 2 Tbsp. canola oil

SALAD

- ½ cup mayonnaise
- 2 Tbsp. grated Parmesan cheese
- 2 Tbsp. lemon juice
- 2 tsp. Dijon mustard
- 2 tsp. Worcestershire sauce
- 2 tsp. anchovy paste
- 1 garlic clove, minced
- ¼ tsp. salt
- ¼ tsp. pepper
- 6 cups torn romaine
- ¼ cup shredded Parmesan cheese

1. Preheat oven to 400°. Place bread in a large bowl. Combine olive oil, garlic salt and pepper; drizzle over bread and toss to coat.
2. Place in a single layer in an ungreased 15x10x1-in. baking pan. Bake until golden brown, 5-7 minutes, stirring occasionally.
3. Meanwhile, sprinkle salmon with salt and pepper. In a large skillet, heat oil over medium heat; add salmon. Cook until salmon just begins to flake easily with a fork, about 5 minutes on each side.
4. In a large bowl, combine mayonnaise, grated Parmesan cheese, lemon juice, Dijon mustard, Worcestershire sauce, anchovy paste, garlic, salt and pepper. Add lettuce, homemade croutons and shredded Parmesan; toss to coat. Divide among 4 plates. Top each with a salmon fillet.

1½ CUPS SALAD WITH 1 SALMON FILLET 616 cal., 49g fat (9g sat. fat), 110mg chol., 1361mg sod., 9g carb. (2g sugars, 2g fiber), 33g pro.

ORIGIN STORY

Caesar salad, the American steakhouse classic, was created in Tijuana, Mexico—by an Italian immigrant! Caesar Cardini cooked up the classic dish in the 1920s at his border-town restaurant that catered to Americans who drove south for wining and dining during American Prohibition. Restaurants in the U.S. added salmon, chicken or steak, taking the famous salad from first course to main event.

BUTTERMILK SOAK

Elk meat is famously lean. Giving it a long soak in buttermilk is the secret weapon for creating tender and juicy, yet still flavorful, steaks.

CHICKEN-FRIED ELK STEAKS

This chicken-fried steak recipe is a delicious way to put elk steaks to use. A buttermilk marinade, a double coating of seasoned flour and white gravy give each bite of meat a lot of flavor and a little crunch!
—Laura Wilhelm

PREP: 35 MIN. + MARINATING
COOK: 20 MIN.
MAKES: 6 SERVINGS

- 6 elk steaks (4 oz. each) (backstrap, hindquarter, or tenderloin)
- 5½ cups buttermilk, divided
- 2 cups all-purpose flour
- 1 Tbsp. Mrs. Dash seasoning blend
- 1 tsp. coarsely ground pepper
- 1 tsp. Hungarian paprika
- ½ tsp. garlic powder
- ½ tsp. onion powder
- ½ tsp. cayenne pepper, optional
- 2 large eggs, beaten
- Oil for deep-fat frying

COUNTRY GRAVY

- ¼ cup all-purpose flour
- 1 tsp. salt
- ½ tsp. coarsely ground pepper
- 3 cups whole milk

1. Rinse the elk steaks in cold water and pat dry. Using a butcher knife, trim off any fat or connective tissue from your steaks as preferred. Cover 1 steak with plastic wrap or parchment. Pound with a meat mallet to ¼-in. thickness. Remove plastic or parchment; repeat with remaining steaks.
2. Pour 4 cups buttermilk into a bowl. Add steaks; refrigerate 4 hours or overnight.
3. Place flour, Mrs. Dash, pepper, paprika, garlic powder, onion powder and, if desired, cayenne pepper into a shallow bowl; whisk to combine. In a separate shallow bowl, whisk remaining 1½ cups buttermilk and eggs until blended.
4. Remove steaks from buttermilk marinade; discard buttermilk. Dip each steak in flour to coat both sides; shake off excess. Dip in egg mixture, then again in flour.
5. In a large cast-iron or other heavy skillet, heat ½ in. oil over medium heat. Add steaks; cook 4-6 minutes on each side or until golden brown and a thermometer reads 135°. Remove from pan; drain on paper towels. Keep warm.
6. For the gravy, remove all but ¼ cup oil from pan. Stir in flour, salt and pepper until smooth; cook and stir over medium heat until golden brown, 3-4 minutes. Gradually whisk in milk. Bring to a boil, stirring constantly; cook and stir until thickened, 1-2 minutes. Serve with steaks.

1 SERVING 326 cal., 9g fat (4g sat. fat), 107mg chol., 602mg sod., 25g carb. (8g sugars, 1g fiber), 34g pro.

THE BEST GRILLED SIRLOIN TIP ROAST

If you're looking for a flavorful cut of meat that's still pretty lean, give this sirloin tip roast recipe a try. I like to cook it slowly over indirect heat, mopping it frequently with red wine sauce.
—James Schend

PREP: 40 MIN. + CHILLING
GRILL: 1½ HOURS + STANDING
MAKES: 6 SERVINGS

- 1 beef sirloin tip roast or beef tri-tip roast (2 to 3 lbs.)
- 1 Tbsp. kosher salt
- 2 tsp. dried thyme
- 2 tsp. garlic powder
- 1 tsp. coarsely ground pepper
- 1 small onion, chopped
- 2 Tbsp. olive oil, divided
- 1 bottle (750 ml) dry red wine
- 6 fresh thyme sprigs
- 1 garlic cloves, crushed
- ½ tsp. whole peppercorns
- 3 whole cloves

HORSERADISH-THYME BUTTER (OPTIONAL)

- 6 Tbsp. softened butter
- 2 Tbsp. prepared horseradish
- 3 Tbsp. fresh thyme leaves

1. Sprinkle roast with salt, thyme, garlic powder and ground pepper. Cover and refrigerate at least 8 hours or up to 24 hours.
2. Meanwhile, in a saucepan, saute onion in 1 Tbsp. oil until tender, about 5 minutes. Add wine, thyme, garlic, peppercorns and cloves. Simmer until reduced to ¾ cup. Cool; strain, discarding solids, and refrigerate.
3. Remove roast from refrigerator 1 hour before grilling. Prepare grill for indirect heat, using a drip pan. Add wood chips according to manufacturer's directions.
4. Pat roast dry with paper towels. Brush with remaining 1 Tbsp. oil; place over drip pan. Grill, covered, over medium-low indirect heat, brushing with red wine sauce every 20 minutes, until meat reaches desired doneness (for medium-rare, a thermometer should read 135°; medium, 140°; medium-well, 145°), 1½-2 hours. Let stand for 15 minutes before slicing.
5. If desired, in a small bowl, stir together butter, horseradish and thyme. Serve on top of roast.

4 OZ. COOKED BEEF 262 cal., 13g fat (4g sat. fat), 91mg chol., 1027mg sod., 3g carb. (1g sugars, 1g fiber), 32g pro.

COLORADO LAMB CHOPS

My mom just loved a good lamb chop, and this easy recipe was her favorite way to make them. I've also grilled these chops with amazing results.
—Kim Mundy

PREP: 10 MIN. + CHILLING
BROIL: 10 MIN.
MAKES: 4 SERVINGS

- **1 tsp. each dried basil, marjoram and thyme**
- **½ tsp. salt**
- **8 lamb loin chops (3 oz. each)**
- **Mint jelly, optional**

1. Combine herbs and salt; rub over lamb chops. Cover and refrigerate for 1 hour.
2. Broil 4-6 in. from the heat until meat reaches desired doneness, 5-8 minutes on each side (for medium-rare, a thermometer should read 135°; medium, 140°; medium-well, 145°). Serve with mint jelly if desired.

2 LAMB CHOPS 157 cal., 7g fat (2g sat. fat), 68mg chol., 355mg sod., 0 carb. (0 sugars, 0 fiber), 22g pro.

HONEY-GLAZED LAMB CHOPS Omit step 1, herbs and salt. In a saucepan, over medium-low heat, cook ⅓ cup each honey and prepared mustard with ⅛ tsp. each onion salt and pepper for 2-3 minutes or until honey is melted. Brush sauce over both sides of lamb. Proceed as directed in step 2.

FROM MOUNTAIN TO MENU

Raised on high-elevation pastures, Colorado lamb develops a naturally mild and sweet flavor. Chefs across the country highlight it on their menus. In Denver restaurants and ski-town steakhouses, simple preparation lets the meat's superior flavors shine.

BISON MEAT LOAF

Since I grew up in Montana, I have been fortunate enough to eat bison meat since childhood. I have always loved it, and I hope you will too!
—Amanda Monroe

PREP: 30 MIN.
BAKE: 50 MIN. + STANDING
MAKES: 8 SERVINGS

- ¾ cup dry bread crumbs
- ¾ cup whole milk
- 1 poblano pepper, seeded and diced
- ¾ cup shredded carrots
- ½ cup chopped onion
- 1 large egg, lightly beaten
- 1 Tbsp. Worcestershire sauce
- 1 tsp. salt
- ½ tsp. pepper
- ½ tsp. ground mustard
- ½ tsp. rubbed sage
- ¼ tsp. celery salt
- ¼ tsp. garlic powder
- 1 lb. ground bison
- 1 lb. ground pork

SAUCE

- ½ cup ketchup
- 1½ tsp. packed brown sugar
- ¾ tsp. white vinegar
- ½ tsp. Worcestershire sauce
- ½ tsp. garlic powder
- ¼ tsp. onion powder
- ¼ tsp. pepper

1. Preheat oven to 350°. In a large bowl, combine first 13 ingredients. Add bison and pork; mix lightly but thoroughly.

2. In a small bowl, combine all sauce ingredients.

3. Shape meat mixture into a loaf about 1½ in. high on a foil-lined rimmed baking sheet. Brush with sauce. Bake until a thermometer reads 160°, 50-60 minutes. Let stand 10 minutes before slicing.

NOTE Wear disposable gloves when cutting hot peppers; the oils can burn skin. Avoid touching your face.

1 SERVING 343 cal., 19g fat (8g sat. fat), 103mg chol., 714mg sod., 17g carb. (8g sugars, 1g fiber), 24g pro.

FUNERAL POTATOES

A friend serves these creamy, cheesy potatoes when we gather to celebrate at holidays.
—*Carol Blue*

PREP: 10 MIN. • **BAKE:** 50 MIN.
MAKES: 12 SERVINGS

- 2 cups sour cream
- 1 can (10¾ oz.) condensed cream of chicken soup, undiluted
- ½ tsp. salt
- ¼ tsp. pepper
- 1 pkg. (30 oz.) frozen shredded hash brown potatoes, thawed
- 2 cups shredded cheddar cheese
- 1 small onion, chopped
- 2 cups crushed cornflakes
- ¼ cup butter, melted

1. Preheat oven to 350°. In a large bowl, mix sour cream, soup, salt and pepper; stir in potatoes, cheese and onion. Transfer to a greased 13x9-in. baking dish.
2. In a small bowl, mix cornflakes and butter; sprinkle over potato mixture. Bake, uncovered, until golden brown, 50-60 minutes.
¾ CUP 394 cal., 22g fat (14g sat. fat), 70mg chol., 680mg sod., 36g carb. (5g sugars, 2g fiber), 11g pro.

READER REVIEW

★★★★★

"I know this recipe as Company Potatoes. I use cream of celery soup instead of chicken. I make this all the time."
—JOYBLACK, TASTEOFHOME.COM

FROG EYE SALAD

As much or as little whipped topping can be added to taste. I use this recipe as a salad, but my friends say it is good enough to be a dessert!
—Elaine Bailey

PREP: 35 MIN. + CHILLING
MAKES: 24 SERVINGS

- 1 cup sugar
- 2 Tbsp. all-purpose flour
- ½ tsp. salt
- 1¾ cups unsweetened pineapple juice
- 2 large eggs, lightly beaten
- 1 Tbsp. lemon juice
- 1 pkg. (16 oz.) acini di pepe pasta
- 3 cans (11 oz. each) mandarin oranges, drained
- 2 cans (20 oz. each) pineapple chunks, drained
- 1 can (20 oz.) crushed pineapple, drained
- 1 cup miniature marshmallows
- 1 cup sweetened shredded coconut
- 1 carton (12 oz.) frozen whipped topping, thawed
- Maraschino cherries, optional

1. In a small saucepan, combine sugar, flour and salt. Gradually stir in pineapple juice. Bring to a boil over medium heat, stirring constantly. Stir a small amount of hot mixture into eggs; return all to the pan, stirring constantly. Bring to a gentle boil; cook and stir 2 minutes longer. Remove from the heat. Gently stir in lemon juice.

2. Transfer to a large bowl. Cool to room temperature without stirring. Cover surface of dressing with waxed paper; refrigerate until cooled.

3. Cook pasta according to the package directions; drain and rinse in cold water. Place in a very large bowl; stir in oranges, pineapple, marshmallows, coconut and dressing. Fold in whipped topping. Cover and refrigerate until chilled. If desired, garnish with cherries.

¾ CUP 240 cal., 5g fat (4g sat. fat), 16mg chol., 72mg sod., 47g carb. (30g sugars, 2g fiber), 4g pro.

HOMEMADE TATER TOTS

If you are a fan of using Tater Tots as a crunchy topping for casseroles, the next step is making your own tots from scratch. It's simple, and once you master the basic technique, you can start experimenting!
—Taste of Home *Test Kitchen*

PREP: 20 MIN.
COOK: 5 MIN./BATCH
MAKES: 6 SERVINGS

- Oil for deep-fat frying
- 2 lbs. russet potatoes, peeled and cut into 1-in. pieces
- 2 Tbsp. minced fresh parsley or 2 tsp. dried parsley flakes
- 1 Tbsp. cornstarch
- 1 tsp. kosher salt
- ½ tsp. onion powder
- ¼ tsp. pepper
- Optional: Sriracha mayonnaise or ranch dressing

1. In an electric skillet or a deep fryer, heat oil to 350°. Place potatoes in a bowl of cold water and stir for 15 seconds. Drain potatoes; pat dry with paper towels. Fry potatoes in batches in oil until lightly browned, 6-8 minutes. Remove with a slotted spoon; drain on paper towels.

2. Increase heat to 375°. In batches, place potatoes in a food processor. Pulse until potatoes are ⅛- to ¼-in. pieces. Transfer to a large bowl. Stir in the remaining ingredients. Shape 1 Tbsp. potato mixture into a 1-in.-long cylinder. Repeat with remaining mixture.

3. Fry tots in oil in batches until crisp and golden brown, 4-5 minutes, turning frequently. Drain on paper towels; serve immediately. If desired, sprinkle with additional salt and minced parsley. Serve with Sriracha mayonnaise or ranch dressing.

FREEZE OPTION Place unfried, shaped tots on a baking sheet; freeze until firm, at least 1 hour. Transfer frozen tots to a freezer container and store for up to 3 months. Fry from frozen in 375° oil until golden brown, 6-8 minutes.

6 TATER TOTS 173 cal., 9g fat (1g sat. fat), 0 chol., 324mg sod., 22g carb. (2g sugars, 2g fiber), 2g pro.

MASHED POTATO DOUGHNUTS

As a special treat in winter, my parents would make a double batch of these doughnuts to welcome us six kids home from school. This recipe from my great-aunt has been handed down through the generations. *—Tammy Evans*

PREP: 20 MIN. + CHILLING
COOK: 5 MIN./BATCH
MAKES: 2 DOZEN

- 1 pkg. (¼ oz.) active dry yeast
- 1 cup warm buttermilk (110°-115°)
- 1½ cups warm mashed potatoes (without added milk and butter)
- 3 large eggs, room temperature
- ⅓ cup butter, melted
- 3 cups sugar, divided
- 4 tsp. baking powder
- 1½ tsp. baking soda
- 1 tsp. salt
- 1 tsp. ground nutmeg
- 6 cups all-purpose flour
- Oil for deep-fat frying
- ½ tsp. ground cinnamon

1. In a large bowl, dissolve yeast in warm buttermilk. Add potatoes, eggs and butter. Add 2 cups sugar, baking powder, baking soda, salt, nutmeg and 3 cups flour. Beat until smooth. Stir in enough remaining flour to form a soft dough. Do not knead. Cover and refrigerate for 2 hours.

2. Turn onto a floured surface; divide into fourths. Roll each portion to ½-in. thickness. Cut with a floured 3-in. doughnut cutter.

3. In an electric skillet or deep-fat fryer, heat the oil to 375°. Fry doughnuts, a few at a time, until golden brown on both sides. Drain on paper towels. Combine the remaining 1 cup sugar and cinnamon; roll doughnuts in cinnamon sugar while warm.

1 DOUGHNUT 295 cal., 8g fat (2g sat. fat), 30mg chol., 309mg sod., 52g carb. (26g sugars, 1g fiber), 5g pro.

INGREDIENT SPOTLIGHT

To many, the big, brown russet potatoes ideal for baking and mashing are synonymous with "Idahos." The state's mineral-rich volcanic soil and chilly nights raise russets with sturdy skins and flavorful, fluffy interiors. Reds, golds and other types are grown in Idaho too.

CAMPFIRE COBBLER

This warm cobbler is one of our favorite ways to end a busy day of fishing, hiking, swimming or rafting. It's yummy with ice cream—and so easy to make!
—June Dress

PREP: 10 MIN. • **GRILL:** 30 MIN.
MAKES: 12 SERVINGS

- 2 cans (21 oz. each) raspberry pie filling
- 1 pkg. yellow cake mix (regular size)
- 1¼ cups water
- ½ cup canola oil
- Vanilla ice cream, optional

1. Prepare grill or campfire for low heat, using 16-20 charcoal briquettes or large wood chips.
2. Line an ovenproof Dutch oven with heavy-duty aluminum foil; add pie filling. In a large bowl, combine the cake mix, water and oil. Spread over pie filling.
3. Place cover on Dutch oven. When briquettes or wood chips are covered with white ash, place Dutch oven directly on top of 8-10 of them. Using long-handled tongs, place remaining briquettes on pot cover.
4. Cook until filling is bubbly and a toothpick inserted in the topping comes out clean, 30-40 minutes. To check for doneness, use the tongs to carefully lift the cover. If desired, serve with ice cream.
1 SERVING 342 cal., 12g fat (2g sat. fat), 0 chol., 322mg sod., 57g carb. (34g sugars, 2g fiber), 1g pro.

SIMPLE LIME GELATIN SALAD

Looking for a colorful dish to light up the buffet? This pretty green gelatin salad has a delightful, tangy flavor to go with its good looks.
—Cyndi Fynaardt

PREP: 20 MIN. + CHILLING
MAKES: 10 SERVINGS

- 2 pkg. (3 oz. each) lime gelatin
- 2 cups boiling water
- 1 qt. lime sherbet
- 1 carton (8 oz.) frozen whipped topping, thawed

1. In a large bowl, dissolve gelatin in boiling water. Beat in sherbet until melted. Add whipped topping; beat well.
2. Pour into an 8-cup ring mold coated with cooking spray. Refrigerate for 4 hours or until set. Unmold onto a serving platter.
1 SERVING 210 cal., 5g fat (4g sat. fat), 0 chol., 66mg sod., 38g carb. (32g sugars, 2g fiber), 2g pro.

JELL-O: FAVORITE SNACK FOOD OF UTAH

Utah is so fond of gelatin salad that lime Jell-O is even jokingly celebrated as the state's favorite snack. Potluck tables and church suppers often feature the wobbly treat whipped up with fruit, grated carrots, marshmallows or creamy additions. Green Jell-O salad is a crowd-pleasing, nostalgic favorite. But is it a side dish or dessert?

APPLE PIE

I remember coming home sullen one day because we'd lost a softball game. Grandma, in her wisdom, suggested, "Maybe a slice of hot apple pie will make you feel better." She was right.
—Maggie Greene

PREP: 20 MIN. • **BAKE:** 1 HOUR
MAKES: 8 SERVINGS

Dough for double-crust pie
- 1/3 cup sugar
- 1/3 cup packed brown sugar
- 1/4 cup all-purpose flour
- 1 tsp. ground cinnamon
- 1/4 tsp. ground ginger
- 1/4 tsp. ground nutmeg
- 6 to 7 cups thinly sliced peeled tart apples
- 1 Tbsp. lemon juice
- 1 Tbsp. butter
- 1 large egg white

Optional: Turbinado or coarse sugar, ground cinnamon, vanilla bean ice cream and caramel sauce

1. Preheat oven to 375°. On a lightly floured surface, roll out half the dough to a 1/8-in.-thick circle; transfer to a 9-in. pie plate. Refrigerate while preparing filling. In a small bowl, combine sugars, flour and spices. In a large bowl, toss apples with lemon juice. Add sugar mixture; toss to coat. Add filling to crust; dot with butter.

2. Roll out remaining dough to a 1/8-in.-thick circle; cut into 1-in.-wide strips. Arrange over filling in a lattice pattern. Trim and seal strips to edge of bottom crust; flute edge. Beat egg white until foamy; brush over crust. If desired, sprinkle with turbinado sugar and cinnamon.

3. Bake on lowest rack until crust is golden brown and filling is bubbly, 60-70 minutes, covering with foil halfway through if crust begins to get too dark. Cool on a wire rack. If desired, serve with ice cream and caramel sauce.

DOUGH FOR DOUBLE-CRUST PIE
Combine 2½ cups all-purpose flour and ½ tsp. salt; cut in 1 cup cold butter until crumbly. Gradually add 1/3-2/3 cup ice water, tossing with a fork until dough holds together when pressed. Divide dough in half. Shape each into a disk; wrap and refrigerate 1 hour.

1 PIECE 467 cal., 25g fat (15g sat. fat), 64mg chol., 331mg sod., 58g carb. (26g sugars, 2g fiber), 5g pro.

CALIFORNIA
QUICK & EASY
CHICKEN POKE
BOWL, P. 117

HAWAII & PACIFIC COAST

Tide-to-table cooking, the Gold Rush expansion and Asian influences leave their stamp in the Pacific Rim, from poke and salmon to tea-smoked dishes and fire-kissed desserts.

MAI TAI

This party favorite has been around for quite some time. It's not overly fruity and features a good blend of sweet and sour. For a splash of color, garnish with strawberries and lime.
—Taste of Home *Test Kitchen*

TAKES: 5 MIN. • **MAKES:** 1 SERVING

- 1½ to 2 cups ice cubes
- 2 oz. light rum
- ¾ oz. triple sec
- ½ oz. lemon juice
- 1½ tsp. lime juice
- 1½ tsp. amaretto
- Optional garnish: Lime slice, lime twist, edible flowers and fresh pineapple

1. Fill a shaker three-fourths full with ice. Place remaining ice in a rocks glass; set aside.
2. Add the rum, triple sec, juices and amaretto to shaker; cover and shake for 10-15 seconds or until condensation forms on outside of shaker. Strain into prepared glass. Garnish as desired.

⅔ CUP 241 cal., 0 fat (0 sat. fat), 0 chol., 7mg sod., 15g carb. (13g sugars, 0 fiber), 0 pro.

ORIGIN STORY

The mai tai, which means "the very best" in Tahitian, may bring to mind gentle ocean breezes and white sand beaches—but it was created in Oakland, at Trader Vic's. In the 1950s, restaurant owner Victor Bergeron introduced it in Hawaii, where it became the state's signature cocktail.

ISLAND-STYLE MAI TAI

The Mai Tai is everywhere in Hawaii—hotel lounges, beach bars and backyard parties—and most spots have a house version. Typical garnishes include a mint sprig, lime wheel and pineapple wedge; some add an orchid, cocktail cherry or a short stick of sugarcane. Many also finish the drink with a float of dark rum on top.

BACON-WRAPPED SPAM BITES

These sweet and savory bites use a favorite ingredient in Hawaii in a fun new way. Bet you can't stop at just one!
—Taste of Home *Test Kitchen*

PREP: 20 MIN. • **BAKE:** 15 MIN.
MAKES: 32 PIECES

- 16 bacon strips
- 1 can (12 oz.) reduced-sodium SPAM, cut into 32 cubes
- 32 wooden toothpicks
- ⅓ cup yellow mustard
- ¼ cup maple syrup
- 1 garlic clove, minced

1. Preheat oven to 400°. Cut bacon strips crosswise in half. In a large skillet, cook bacon over medium heat until partially cooked but not crisp. Remove to paper towels to drain; keep warm.
2. Wrap a bacon piece around each Spam cube; secure with a toothpick. Place in a 15x10x1-in. ungreased baking pan. Bake for 10 minutes. In a bowl, combine mustard, syrup and garlic; drizzle over bacon-wrapped Spam. Bake until bacon is crisp, 5-10 minutes longer.
1 PIECE 60 cal., 4g fat (1g sat. fat), 12mg chol., 211mg sod., 2g carb. (2g sugars, 0 fiber), 3g pro.

CRAB LOUIE LETTUCE WRAPS

Party guests can mingle and enjoy these tasty hand-held lettuce wraps without the fear of balancing plates and forks.
—*Michael Watz*

TAKES: 30 MIN.
MAKES: 12 SERVINGS

- 1 cup sour cream
- ½ cup sweet chili sauce
- 2 Tbsp. minced fresh gingerroot
- 1 Tbsp. lime juice
- ¼ tsp. ground cumin
- 1 can (6 oz.) lump crabmeat, drained and squeezed dry
- 12 Bibb or Boston lettuce leaves
- 2 medium mangoes, peeled and thinly sliced
- 2 medium ripe avocados, peeled and thinly sliced
- 4 green onions, thinly sliced
- 1 medium carrot, shredded
- ¼ cup fresh cilantro leaves
- ¼ cup fresh mint leaves, chopped if desired
- 2 Tbsp. toasted sesame seeds

1. In a small bowl, mix the first 5 ingredients.
2. To serve, place about 1 Tbsp. crabmeat in each lettuce leaf. Top with remaining ingredients. Drizzle with some of the sauce. Serve with remaining sauce.
1 FILLED LETTUCE WRAP WITH ABOUT 2 TBSP. SAUCE 160 cal., 9g fat (3g sat. fat), 25mg chol., 240mg sod., 16g carb. (12g sugars, 4g fiber), 5g pro.

BLACKBERRY SPINACH SALAD

This lightly dressed salad is packed with superfoods! When I have time, I make my vinaigrette from scratch. *—Mary Lou Timpson*

TAKES: 15 MIN.
MAKES: 6 SERVINGS

- 3 cups fresh baby spinach
- 2 cups fresh blackberries, halved
- 1½ cups cherry tomatoes, halved
- ⅓ cup crumbled feta cheese
- 2 green onions, thinly sliced
- ¼ cup chopped walnuts, toasted
- ⅓ cup balsamic vinaigrette

In a large bowl, combine the first 6 ingredients. Divide salad among 6 plates; drizzle with dressing.
1 CUP 106 cal., 7g fat (1g sat. fat), 3mg chol., 230mg sod., 9g carb. (4g sugars, 4g fiber), 3g pro.

INGREDIENT SPOTLIGHT

Oregon blackberries taste like summer turned up to 11. Cool nights and mild days let them ripen slowly for big perfume and pop. In August, the Willamette Valley brims with berries, both commercially grown and wild. Most blackberries we eat in the U.S. hail from here.

SALMON WITH BROWN SUGAR GLAZE

Need a simple way to serve a whole salmon fillet to a group of friends? Here's the super easy recipe that finally made me a fan of this fish. *—Rachel Garcia*

PREP: 15 MIN. • **BAKE:** 20 MIN.
MAKES: 8 SERVINGS

- 1 Tbsp. brown sugar
- 2 tsp. butter
- 1 tsp. honey
- 1 Tbsp. olive oil
- 1 Tbsp. Dijon mustard
- 1 Tbsp. reduced-sodium soy sauce
- ½ to ¾ tsp. salt
- ¼ tsp. pepper
- 1 salmon fillet (2½ lbs.)

1. In a small saucepan over medium heat, cook and stir brown sugar, butter and honey until melted. Remove from heat; whisk in oil, mustard, soy sauce, salt and pepper. Cool for 5 minutes.
2. Place salmon in a large foil-lined baking pan; spoon brown sugar mixture over top. Bake at 350° for 20-25 minutes or until fish flakes easily with a fork.
1 SERVING 295 cal., 18g fat (3g sat. fat), 84mg chol., 403mg sod., 3g carb. (2g sugars, 0 fiber), 28g pro.

QUICK & EASY CHICKEN POKE BOWL

This poke bowl is a great alternative when sushi-grade fish isn't in the budget. I love it because it's quick, easy and inexpensive. While it's not a traditional poke recipe, the chicken still rocks in this bowl.
—*Emily Cresta*

PREP: 25 MIN. + CHILLING
COOK: 5 MIN. • **MAKES:** 4 SERVINGS

- 1 cup uncooked sushi (short grain) rice

PICKLED ONIONS

- ½ cup cider vinegar
- 1 Tbsp. sugar
- 1 small red onion, thinly sliced

SPICY MAYONNAISE

- ⅓ cup mayonnaise
- 4 tsp. Sriracha chili sauce

POKE BOWL

- 2 cups shredded rotisserie chicken
- 2 Tbsp. reduced-sodium soy sauce
- 2 tsp. toasted sesame oil
- 1 tsp. honey
- 1 medium ripe avocado, peeled and sliced
- ½ small cucumber, thinly sliced
- 1 cup alfalfa or bean sprouts
- Optional: Sliced green onions and sesame seeds

1. Cook rice according to package directions. Meanwhile, in a resealable jar, whisk vinegar and sugar until dissolved; add red onion. Seal and refrigerate 30 minutes or up to 2 weeks. In a small bowl, stir together mayonnaise and chili sauce; refrigerate, covered, until serving.

2. In a large skillet or wok, toss chicken, soy sauce, sesame oil and honey. Cook and stir over medium-low heat until chicken is heated through, 5-7 minutes. To serve, divide rice among 4 serving bowls. Top with chicken mixture, avocado, cucumber, sprouts, pickled onions, spicy mayonnaise and, if desired, green onions and sesame seeds.

1 BOWL 539 cal., 26g fat (5g sat. fat), 64mg chol., 606mg sod., 49g carb. (4g sugars, 4g fiber), 25g pro.

READER REVIEW

★★★★★

"This was super. DH and I devoured it. I forgot to buy sprouts, and I opted for chopped dry-roasted peanuts over sesame seeds; otherwise I prepared it as directed in the recipe. It was the perfect use for leftover takeout rice too!"

—BROWNS19FAN, TASTEOFHOME.COM

SAN FRANCISCO CIOPPINO

Traditionally, cioppino is made with whatever seafood was caught that day or whatever seafood is on hand. It began as a soup for the working class, but with how delicious it tastes, it's no wonder this dish made its way into high-end restaurants and hotels. Feel free to use whatever fish, shellfish and seafood you can find.
—Barbara Pletzke

PREP: 35 MIN. • **COOK:** 50 MIN.
MAKES: 8 SERVINGS (4 QT.)

- 2 Tbsp. olive oil
- 1 medium fennel bulb, thinly sliced
- 1 shallot, minced
- 3 garlic cloves, minced
- 6 fresh thyme sprigs
- 2 fresh rosemary sprigs
- 2 Tbsp. minced fresh parsley
- ½ tsp. crushed red pepper flakes
- 2 cans (15 oz. each) crushed tomatoes, undrained
- 2 bottles (8 oz. each) clam juice
- 1 cup dry red wine
- ½ tsp. salt
- ½ tsp. freshly ground pepper
- 16 fresh topneck clams
- 16 fresh mussels, scrubbed and beards removed
- 16 uncooked shrimp (26-30 per lb.), peeled and deveined
- 1 lb. halibut fillets, cut into 1-in. cubes
- 16 snow crab claws
- 16 bay scallops
- 2 cleaned fresh or frozen calamari (squid) tubes, thawed and sliced into ⅛-in. rings (about 2 oz.)
- 4 Tbsp. anise liqueur, such as sambuca
- Additional minced fresh parsley

1. In a Dutch oven, heat oil over medium-high heat. Add fennel; cook until crisp-tender, 2-3 minutes. Add shallot and garlic; cook for 1 minute longer. Add the thyme, rosemary, parsley and red pepper flakes; cook 1 minute longer. Stir in tomatoes, clam juice, wine, salt and pepper. Bring to a boil. Reduce heat; simmer, uncovered, for 20 minutes. Discard herb stems.

2. Add the clams, mussels and shrimp. Bring to a boil. Reduce heat; simmer, uncovered, for 4 minutes, stirring occasionally. Stir in halibut; cook 3 minutes. Add crab claws, scallops and calamari; cook until clams and mussels open, shrimp turn pink and scallops are opaque, 5-7 minutes longer. Discard any unopened clams or mussels.

3. Serve in bowls; top with liqueur and additional minced parsley.

2 CUPS 298 cal., 8g fat (1g sat. fat), 140mg chol., 830mg sod., 15g carb. (6g sugars, 3g fiber), 35g pro.

WHARFSIDE WARMER-UPPER

Created on the wharf, this stew flexes with the catch, using shrimp, mussels, clams, firm white fish and sometimes crab. Fennel, garlic and tomatoes are popular. Some cooks add saffron too: Bloom it in a small amount of warm clam juice or wine and stir it in at the end for a golden, floral lift. This San Francisco classic was made for dipping with sourdough.

HAWAIIAN FRIED RICE

Growing up in the South Pacific, rice was the mainstay of our diet. When my husband and I moved stateside, we created this recipe. We bring this dish to every potluck, and it's always the hit of the party.
—Janice Edwards

PREP: 25 MIN. • **COOK:** 20 MIN.
MAKES: 8 SERVINGS

- 3 cups uncooked long grain rice
- 10 Tbsp. margarine or butter, divided
- 8 large eggs
- 1 can (12 oz.) lite SPAM, cut into ¼-in. cubes
- ⅓ cup chopped onion
- 4 cups frozen mixed vegetables (about 16 oz.), thawed and drained
- 2 garlic cloves, minced
- ½ tsp. pepper
- ⅓ cup soy sauce
- Sliced green onions, optional

1. Cook rice according to package directions. Meanwhile, in a Dutch oven, heat 1 Tbsp. margarine over medium-high heat. Whisk eggs until blended; pour into pan. Mixture should set immediately at edge. As eggs set, push cooked portions toward center, letting uncooked portions flow underneath. When eggs are thickened and no liquid egg remains, remove to a cutting board and chop.

2. In same pan, heat 1 Tbsp. margarine over medium-high heat. Add Spam and onion; cook and stir until Spam is lightly browned, 6-8 minutes. Add mixed vegetables, garlic and pepper; cook until heated through. Stir in cooked rice, soy sauce and the remaining ½ cup margarine; cook and stir until margarine is melted. Gently stir in eggs. If desired, top with sliced green onion.

1¾ CUPS 621 cal., 24g fat (6g sat. fat), 220mg chol., 1191mg sod., 74g carb. (4g sugars, 5g fiber), 24g pro.

FARMERS MARKET STREET TACOS

No matter what I find at San Diego's Hillcrest Farmers Market, I always end up stuffing it into a taco for a fresh veggie-filled treat. You really can't go wrong.
—Ralph Jones

TAKES: 30 MIN.
MAKES: 4 SERVINGS

- 2 bunches bok choy, halved
- 1 medium zucchini, cut into 3-in. sticks
- ½ lb. fresh asparagus spears
- 2 medium ripe avocados, peeled and quartered
- 1 bunch green onions
- 2 jalapeno peppers, halved and seeded
- 2 Tbsp. olive oil
- ½ tsp. kosher salt
- ½ tsp. pepper
- 8 mini corn tortillas
- Fresh cilantro leaves
- Optional: Pickled red onions, lime wedges, sliced radishes and salsa verde

1. Prepare grill for medium-high heat. Brush bok choy, zucchini, asparagus, avocados, green onions and jalapenos with olive oil; sprinkle with salt and pepper. Transfer to a greased grill rack.
2. Grill, covered, or broil 4 in. from heat until vegetables are crisp-tender and slightly charred, 4-5 minutes, turning occasionally. Grill tortillas until warmed and slightly charred, 30-45 seconds per side. Cut vegetables to desired sizes; serve in tortillas with cilantro and toppings of your choice.

NOTE Wear disposable gloves when cutting hot peppers; the oils can burn skin. Avoid touching your face.

2 TACOS 319 cal., 19g fat (3g sat. fat), 0 chol., 536mg sod., 33g carb. (9g sugars, 13g fiber), 11g pro.

DID YOU KNOW?

Avocado is high in monounsaturated fat, a so-called "good fat" that can lower your blood cholesterol along with the risk of stroke and heart disease. Each fruit also contains about 9 grams of healthy fiber.

TEA-SMOKED CHICKEN

This whole chicken is simmered in an aromatic soy-based broth, then smoked. A mixture of rice, tea leaves and brown sugar is used to smoke this traditional Peking-style chicken, giving it a distinct flavor.
—May Der

PREP: 20 MIN. + CHILLING
COOK: 70 MIN. + STANDING
MAKES: 6 SERVINGS

- 3 Tbsp. Sichuan peppercorns
- 3 Tbsp. salt
- 1 whole broiler/fryer chicken (4 to 5 lbs.)
- 8 cups water
- 1 cup reduced-sodium soy sauce
- 2 green onions, sliced
- 3 slices fresh gingerroot
- 2 whole star anise
- 1 cinnamon stick (3 in.)
- 1 tsp. Chinese five-spice powder
- ½ cup uncooked long grain rice
- ½ cup loose black tea leaves
- ½ cup packed brown sugar
- 1 tsp. sesame oil

1. Place peppercorns in a spice grinder or a mortar and pestle; grind until coarsely ground. Place peppercorns and salt in a dry small skillet; toast over medium heat for 1-2 minutes or until aromatic, stirring occasionally. Cool completely.
2. Pat chicken dry; rub peppercorn mixture over the outside and inside of chicken. Cover and refrigerate for at least 4 hours or overnight.
3. In a stockpot, combine the water, soy sauce, green onions, ginger, star anise, cinnamon stick and five-spice powder; bring to a boil. Reduce heat; simmer, uncovered, for 10 minutes.
4. Add chicken. Return to a boil. Reduce heat; simmer, covered, for 35-40 minutes or until a thermometer inserted in thigh reads 180°, turning chicken once. Remove chicken; discard cooking liquid.
5. Line the bottom of a clean stockpot with a double thickness of foil. Sprinkle the rice, tea leaves and brown sugar over foil; place a wire rack over rice mixture. Place chicken on rack breast side up.
6. Cook over low heat until rice mixture begins to smoke. Cover pot tightly with foil; place lid on top. Smoke for 25-30 minutes or until chicken is golden brown.
7. Remove chicken; brush with sesame oil. Let stand 15 minutes before carving. Chicken may also be served cold. To serve cold, cool chicken slightly; cover and refrigerate until chilled.

5 OZ. COOKED CHICKEN401 cal., 23g fat (6g sat. fat), 139mg chol., 745mg sod., 0 carb. (0 sugars, 0 fiber), 44g pro.

CALIFORNIA CHINESE COOKING

Chinese—mostly Cantonese—immigrants arrived in San Francisco in the 1840s and soon adapted their traditional dishes for Gold Rush appetites. Many restaurants ran two menus, one in the native language and one in English with a new Chinese-American cooking style. Crisp and glossy "Peking-style" tea-smoked chicken and duck became a staple in Los Angeles and San Francisco, as did sweet-and-sour pork and chicken. These innovations gave rise to what Americans know as Chinese cooking today.

RHUBARB CRISP

I found this recipe on a box of Quaker Oats about 20 years ago. It's quick and easier to make than pie. It's versatile, too, because you can add strawberries in spring or apples in fall. I usually pop it into the oven shortly before we sit down to eat so we can enjoy it warm for dessert!
—C.E. Adams

PREP: 15 MIN. • **BAKE:** 45 MIN.
MAKES: 8 SERVINGS

- ¾ cup sugar
- 3 Tbsp. cornstarch
- 3 cups sliced fresh rhubarb or frozen rhubarb, thawed
- 2 cups sliced peeled apples or sliced strawberries
- 1 cup quick-cooking or old-fashioned oats
- ½ cup packed brown sugar
- ½ cup butter, melted
- ⅓ cup all-purpose flour
- 1 tsp. ground cinnamon
- Vanilla ice cream, optional

1. In a large bowl, combine sugar and cornstarch. Add rhubarb and apples or strawberries; toss to coat. Spoon into an 8-in. cast-iron skillet or other ovenproof skillet.

2. In a small bowl, combine oats, brown sugar, butter, flour and cinnamon until mixture resembles coarse crumbs. Sprinkle over the fruit. Bake at 350° until crisp is bubbly and fruit is tender, about 45 minutes. Serve warm, with ice cream if desired.

1 CUP 320 cal., 12g fat (7g sat. fat), 31mg chol., 124mg sod., 52g carb. (36g sugars, 3g fiber), 3g pro.

INGREDIENT SPOTLIGHT

Part veggie, part fruity-tasting harbinger of spring, rhubarb snaps like celery when raw and turns silken and mellow when cooked. It thrives in cool weather, and the Pacific Northwest—especially Washington's Pierce County from Tacoma to Rainier—grows the most in America. Rhubarb is best with lots sugar and a fruity sidekick—strawberries are a classic pairing.

MINTY BAKED ALASKA

Can you believe it? This stunning dessert is completely make ahead, including the meringue. All you need to do is bake it for a few minutes in the oven before serving.
—Taste of Home *Test Kitchen*

PREP: 45 MIN. + FREEZING
BAKE: 5 MIN. • **MAKES:** 12 SERVINGS

- ½ cup butter, cubed
- 2 oz. unsweetened chocolate, chopped
- 1 cup sugar
- 1 tsp. vanilla extract
- 2 large eggs, room temperature
- ¾ cup all-purpose flour
- ½ tsp. baking powder
- ½ tsp. salt
- 2 qt. vanilla ice cream, softened
- 1 pkg. (4.67 oz.) mint Andes candies, chopped
- 2 Tbsp. creme de menthe
- 1 Tbsp. creme de cacao
- Green food coloring, optional

MERINGUE

- 8 large egg whites
- 1 cup sugar
- 1 tsp. cream of tartar

1. In a microwave-safe bowl, melt the butter and chocolate; stir until smooth. Stir in sugar. Beat in vanilla and eggs, 1 at a time, beating well after each addition. Combine flour, baking powder and salt; stir into chocolate mixture.

2. Transfer to a greased 8-in. round baking pan. Bake at 350° for 30-35 minutes or until a toothpick inserted in the center comes out with moist crumbs (do not overbake). Cool for 10 minutes before removing from pan to a wire rack to cool completely.

3. Meanwhile, in a large bowl, combine the ice cream, Andes candies, liqueurs and, if desired, food coloring. Transfer to an 8-in. round bowl (1½ qt.) lined with plastic wrap; freeze until set.

4. In a large heavy saucepan, combine the egg whites, sugar and cream of tartar. With a hand mixer, beat on low speed for 1 minute. Continue beating over low heat until egg mixture reaches 160°, about 8 minutes. Transfer to a bowl; beat until stiff glossy peaks form and sugar is dissolved.

5. Place brownie on an ungreased foil-lined baking sheet; top with inverted ice cream mold. Remove plastic wrap. Immediately spread meringue over ice cream, sealing to edge of brownie. Freeze until ready to serve, up to 24 hours.

6. Bake at 400° for 2-5 minutes or until meringue is lightly browned, or use a kitchen torch to carefully toast the meringue. Transfer to a serving plate; serve immediately.

1 PIECE 523 cal., 24g fat (16g sat. fat), 94mg chol., 294mg sod., 70g carb. (57g sugars, 1g fiber), 9g pro.

FIRE & ICE IN THE LAST FRONTIER

They call it Baked Alaska, but the name was minted a world away—at Delmonico's in New York City in the 1870s, presumably to celebrate the Alaska Purchase. Tourists still seek out the specialty today—especially in Anchorage—where some ice cream parlors even craft the "Baked Alaska cone" by piping marshmallowy meringue over an ice cream cone and giving it a quick flame-broiled kiss.

PATRIOTIC BERRY CREAM TART

Here's a star-spangled tart to put everyone in a celebratory mood. The filling mounds and swoops in this fluffy creation.
—*Sarah Farmer, Waukesha, WI*

PREP: 25 MIN.
BAKE: 15 MIN. + CHILLING
MAKES: 8 SERVINGS

- 22 Oreo cookies
- 5 Tbsp. butter, melted
- 1 envelope unflavored gelatin
- ¼ cup cold water
- 2 pkg. (8 oz. each) cream cheese, softened
- ½ cup sugar
- 2 cups heavy whipping cream
- 2 tsp. vanilla extract or paste
- Raspberries and blueberries
- Optional: White candy coating stars

1. Preheat oven to 350°. Pulse cookies in a food processor until finely ground. Add butter; pulse until blended. Press mixture into a greased 9-in. tart pan. Bake 15 minutes. Cool completely on a wire rack.

2. Meanwhile, sprinkle gelatin over cold water; let stand for 5 minutes. Beat the cream cheese and sugar until smooth. Slowly beat in cream and vanilla. Microwave the gelatin mixture on high until melted, about 10 seconds; beat into the cream cheese mixture. Transfer filling to crust. Refrigerate, covered, until set, about 3 hours.

3. Remove tart from pan. Top with berries and, if desired, candy coating stars.

1 PIECE 668 cal., 55g fat (32g sat. fat), 144mg chol., 377mg sod., 40g carb. (29g sugars, 1g fiber), 7g pro.

INSTA-WORTHY PIECES

For picture-perfect pieces, dip a knife in hot water, wipe it dry on a clean towel, then quickly cut with the hot knife.

INDEX